GLOBAL CITIZENSHIP

Being Active Citizens

SUSAN WATSON

This edition first published in 2004 in the United States of America by Smart Apple Media.

Smart Apple Media
1980 Lookout Drive
North Mankato
Minnesota 56003

Library of Congress Cataloging-in-Publication Data

Watson, Susan, 1949–
   Being active citizens / by Susan Watson.
   p. cm. — (Global citizenship)

   Includes index.
   Contents: Young people as citizens—Relating to others as citizens—Rights and responsibilities—Active citizens think about issues—Citizens in the global system—Global issues for global citizens—Making global connections—Global citizens make a difference.

   ISBN 1-58340-398-1
   1. International relations—Citizen participation—Juvenile literature. 2. World citizenship—Juvenile literature.
   [1. World citizenship. 2. Globalization. 3. Conduct of life.] I. Title.
   JZ1242.W38 2003
   323.6—dc21   2002044625

First Edition
9 8 7 6 5 4 3 2 1

First published in 2003 by
MACMILLAN EDUCATION AUSTRALIA PTY LTD
627 Chapel Street, South Yarra, Australia 3141

Associated companies and representatives throughout the world.

Packaged for Macmillan Education Australia by Publishing Options Pty Ltd
Text design by Gail McManus Graphics
Cover design by Dimitrios Frangoulis
Illustrations by Infographics Pty Ltd
Page make-up by Crackerjack Desktop Services

Printed in Thailand

Acknowledgements
The author is especially grateful to Matthew, Kyja, CJ, and Samantha for being the model global citizens of this series. The author and the publisher are grateful to the following for permission to reproduce copyright materials:

Cover photograph: cultural festival, courtesy of Coo-ee Picture Library.

ANT Photo Library, p. 23 (left); Jean-Paul Ferrero/Auscape International, p. 17 (top); Kevin Hamdorf/Auscape International, p. 16; Australian Antarctic Division, p. 22 (top); Clean Up Australia Ltd, p. 13 (top); Stewart Collins, p. 28; Coo-ee Picture Library, pp. 4–5 (center), 6, 9, 11 (top), 12, 15, 20 (left), 24 (top); Getty Images, pp. 7 (top), 8, 14, 19, 20 (top), 20 (bottom right), 21 (bottom), 21 (top right), 21 (center right), 25 (left); The G.R. "Dick" Roberts Photo Library, p. 23 (top right); Pelusey Photography, p. 21 (top left); Reuters, p. 26; Salvation Army, p. 27 (bottom); South Australian Museum, p. 25 (top right); Susan Watson, pp. 4 (far left), 4 (center left), 5 (center right), 5 (far right), 30; World Vision, pp. 27 (top), 29.

Please note
At the time of printing, the Internet addresses appearing in this book were correct. Owing to the dynamic nature of the Internet, however, we cannot guarantee that all these addresses will remain correct.

Contents

Global citizens

citizen
a person living in a larger group of people who they mix with

rights
fair claims to things in daily life

responsibilities
duties that have to be done

environments
natural and built surroundings

action
something that a person does and the way they do it

A global citizen is a person who:

◎ has rights and responsibilities
◎ acts in a caring way based on knowledge and understanding
◎ relates to others within their family, friendship groups, community, and country
◎ develops personal values and commitments
◎ develops a sense of their own role in the world.

A study of global citizenship will help you understand how people affect the quality of global environments and the well-being of others. Active global citizens do not just sit back and wait for others to do something. They turn their ideas into action. Action can take many forms:

◎ volunteering by giving time, help, and ideas freely
◎ talking to your friends
◎ thinking deeply
◎ learning more
◎ taking part in community events.

Throughout this book Allira, Harry, Lin, and Denzel will tell you their ways of acting as global citizens. We can all care for each other and our environment.

ALLIRA

Hi! I'm Allira. I live in a country town near the sea. My family background is Aboriginal–Australian.

HARRY

Hello. I'm Harry. I live with my family in a suburb of a big modern city of four million people.

we are global citizens

Everyone is a citizen. We are citizens of:
◎ the local neighborhood
◎ a state, county, or province
◎ a country
◎ the wider world.
People are citizens because they live together in groups. People mix with each other every day:
◎ in their neighborhood
◎ at school
◎ in community activities
◎ at work.
People can listen to what is happening around them. They can watch events unfolding on the TV news or read about them in newspapers. They can choose to do nothing about them.

However, some people think more deeply about things. They have ideas about the events that are happening around them. They become active citizens by turning their ideas into actions. Active citizens are involved with the things happening around them in their local community and the wider world.

We are global citizens

LIN

I'm Lin. I migrated to my new country with my parents. We live with my grandparents who came 15 years ago from Malaysia.

DENZEL

Hi! I'm Denzel. My mom and I live in a high-rise apartment close to the city center. We're African-American.

We are all citizens. We have the right to meet and discuss ideas. We can take part in events together.

Your identity

Everybody has an individual identity. Your identity is what makes you who you are. It is the way you think and act. Your identity sets you apart from every other person in the world. It is your personality. Your identity shapes how you behave.

Your name tells other people what to call you. As they get to know you, they think about who you are. People connect your name with your personality.

People have different identities. Some people have strong personalities. They may be good talkers and involved in lots of activities. Other people are shy and very quiet.

identity
a person's own character

self-esteem
the opinion you have of yourself

Your self-esteem

We all think about ourselves in a particular way. We have self-esteem or personal feelings, such as:
◎ "I'm a good runner and my family is proud of me."
◎ "I'm happy when I'm helping people."
◎ "I leave my room in a mess most days. I'm sloppy."
These questions will help you think about your own identity and self-esteem:
◎ What is my name?
◎ What is my personality like?
◎ How do I act towards others?
◎ How do others see me?
◎ What is my self-esteem like?

We are all individuals with our own personalities. We think about ourselves in a particular way. We all have our own identity and self-esteem.

Your ideas

Everybody has their own ideas. They are personal opinions. Ideas are formed from the things you know or think you know. Ideas can be influenced by:

◎ your family and friends
◎ your cultural group
◎ TV programs and movies
◎ the news
◎ the books, newspapers, and magazines you read
◎ what you see around you
◎ listening to older people such as teachers, church leaders, and politicians.

Your ideas help you make up your mind or form an opinion about something. This might be something simple, such as where to go for vacation. Or it could be harder, like coming up with some ideas to help poor people.

People in your family help shape your ideas.

Your actions

Having ideas often leads to some sort of action. Some people believe that "actions speak louder than words." This means that when you act on your ideas you are doing something about what you think. You might have the idea that you could give one hour each week to helping an older person by keeping them company. It is only when you do this that your idea turns into action.

Action helps shape an individual as a citizen. Citizens' actions affect other people. They can have a good result, but sometimes they can be harmful.

People who act on their ideas are sometimes viewed by others as being forceful. However, standing up for what you believe in can be done in a peaceful way. A forceful person can act on their ideas without being violent.

What can I do?

Lately, I've been feeling sorry for myself and a bit lazy, so I've decided to join my local sports club. I'll meet some new friends there and get better at running. I want my mom and dad to be proud of me.

Your family

The first group that an individual belongs to is the family. A family consists of parents and their children, but can also include other relatives. Some children do not have a blood tie to the parents because they joined the family through adoption or fostering.

From an early age, your family is the most important influence on your identity. You learn ways of thinking and behaving from your family members. This influences how you will act as a citizen as you get older.

adoption
to take someone else's child legally into a new family

fostering
to care for someone else's child within a different family

Different types of families

Throughout your local area and the wider world there are a range of different family structures. Some of these include:

◎ the nuclear family, which consists of a mother, father, and their children

◎ the extended family, which is larger than the nuclear family and includes other relatives such as grandparents, aunts, uncles, and cousins

◎ single-parent families, where only one parent lives with the children

◎ blended families, where members of at least two previous family groups live together. A parent with a child marrying another parent with a child is a blended family.

The family group influences a person's identity from an early age.

Your friends

As well as your family, you belong to a group of friends or a peer group. This group also influences the opinions you form and how you act as a citizen.

Friends can be neighbors who you play with. You make friends at school and in after-school groups.

Friendships can also extend beyond the neighborhood. More and more young people use the Internet to keep in touch with a wide circle of friends. Friendship groups like this help you widen the groups you relate to so that you start to think and act as a global citizen.

peer group
friends and others you mix with of about the same age

Friends and the school community help shape ideas and actions.

Your community

Another important influence on being a citizen is the community. We all participate in a community in one way or another. We have to follow the customs and rules within our community, such as how to relate to older people or how to dispose of our trash.

In the school community you learn to relate to others in your class, to your teachers, to students in other classes, to some of the parents of your friends, and to other staff members. In your neighborhood community you learn to relate to the families who live around you and to a range of other people, such as storekeepers, police officers, and community workers.

The contact that individuals have with their community helps shape the ideas and actions that make them citizens.

customs
the usual ways of doing things

Your place in your nation

It is important for citizens to know about the history (past) and geography (place) of the nation that they are part of. The history of a nation gives clues about how citizens lived in the past, and how society has changed over time. Geography helps locate a place in the world. It provides facts about the country, such as population, climate, government, and how people live.

Active citizens are people who can talk to others about their nation in an informed way.

nation

a large number of people living in a country under the same government

National identity

Just like a person, a nation also has an identity. Every nation has its own flag and other emblems that show its national identity. Flags are displayed on occasions where large groups of people gather, such as school assemblies, sports and cultural events, and memorial days. Emblems are used on buildings and documents that have national importance, such as government buildings or published laws.

Another way that a nation identifies itself is through the national anthem. Citizens show their pride in and loyalty to their country by singing the anthem at public events.

The national flags and emblems of three nations of the world—from left to right, the United States, South Africa, and Fiji. Flags and emblems are part of a nation's identity.

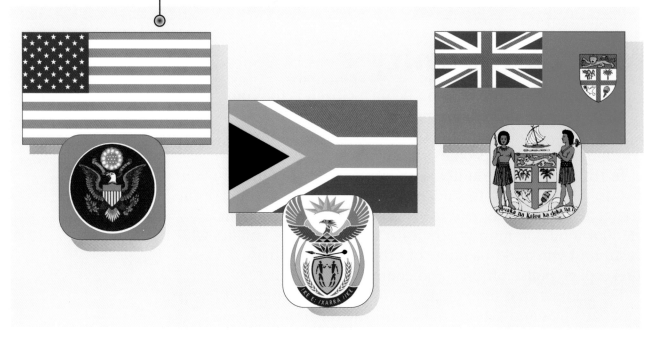

Your place in the world

There are some things that people of the world have in common:

◎ They share things in nature, such as air, water, oceans, and polar lands.
◎ They belong to a group that is part of a nation and the world.
◎ Each nation is part of the global family of nations.
◎ Many parents want their children to have lives better than their own.
◎ They want to live in peace and safety.
◎ Most are concerned about the effect that they have on the environment.

Although people share things in common, the world is also a very complex place made up of different:

◎ environments
◎ customs and practices
◎ types of government
◎ religions
◎ languages
◎ types of families
◎ levels of wealth and well-being of people.

It is important that many of these differences exist. They are part of the world's diversity. But it is also important to help improve the things that are harmful to the environment and to other people.

Global citizens are aware and active. They can help improve life on Earth by:

◎ reducing the destruction of the natural environment
◎ working to help all people have a fair and comfortable life.

Citizens often group together to help protect the globe.

GLOBAL FACT

There are about 195 separate nations in the world.

wealth
the amount of money and resources that a person or country has

well-being
the situation of being happy, healthy, and comfortable

diversity
the range of different things

What can I do?
I want to know more about the history and geography of my country. I'll do some research in the library and on the Internet. I'll also talk to Grandpa—he knows a lot.

Rights and responsibilities

The rights of citizens

Rights are the things that people are entitled to as part of living in a community. Some of the basic rights of citizens are:

◎ freedom of speech and movement
◎ to be protected from harm
◎ to live comfortably
◎ to elect the members of the country's government
◎ to take part in community activities
◎ to own property
◎ to have their own religion or special beliefs
◎ to work and be paid fairly
◎ to be treated equally by the people and laws of the country.

Democracies usually give all these rights to their citizens.

freedom
not being controlled by others

elect
to choose someone for a position by voting

democracies
countries where the government is freely elected by all the people

exploit
to use selfishly and for personal gain

These people are voting on election day in a democracy.

CASE STUDY Children have special rights

Children are important because they will take their ideas and actions into the future. Children need care and protection so that they can grow into good citizens. Many countries give young people some extra rights because of their age and inexperience. Some of these children's rights are:

• the right to love, understanding, and a family group in which to live
• the right to play freely
• the right to go to school until they are about 15 years old
• the right to be paid for part-time work
• the right to be protected from adults who want to harm or exploit them.

The responsibilities of citizens

Citizens also have responsibilities. There are duties they need to do as part of being a member of a family, community, or nation.

There is a popular saying: "You can't have one without the other." This applies to the responsibilities of being a citizen. For people to have the rights of citizenship, they must be prepared to accept the responsibilities that go with them.

Right	Responsibility
To be able to play and enjoy sports.	To balance the amount of time spent playing and having a good time with other activities such as going to school and doing jobs around the house.
To be able to drink freshwater.	To use water wisely and avoid wasteful practices such as leaving faucets on or watering in the middle of the day.
To live in a community and share its benefits.	To be loyal to the country in which you live.
To be protected from harm.	To avoid harming other people.
To be treated equally and fairly.	To treat others equally and fairly regardless of their background or beliefs.
To be able to walk in and enjoy nature.	To take care not to damage plants, animals, and other creatures in the natural environment.

Everyone has a responsibility as a citizen to dispose of trash in a way that will not damage the environment.

What can I do?

As a citizen, I have the right to own my pet dog. I also have the responsibility of caring for him. I have to feed him, give him a clean, warm place to sleep, and take him for walks.

values
the ideas and
behavior that a
group wants its
members to follow

ideals
something to
aim for

respect
a high opinion
of someone
or something

Values in active citizenship

Many of our responsibilities are based on the values of the groups in which we live, play, and work. Values tell us what a society regards as "good," "desirable," "fair," and "decent." They are the high ideals that many people aim for in their lives. People display these values in different ways. They could be day-to-day situations, such as volunteering to help people less fortunate or less able. They could be bigger events, such as rescues, disasters, or war.

Honesty

Honesty is telling the truth, and not cheating or stealing. An honest person does not deliberately hide the facts, cheat, or steal. Global citizens are honest with themselves and with others. They value honesty.

Compassion

Compassion is an emotion or feeling. Showing you feel sorry for someone because they are not as happy or fortunate as you is compassion. Compassion helps people think about others and not only themselves. Compassionate people accept others, even if their views are different.

Respect

When you consider something carefully and value it, you are showing respect. You can show respect towards the laws of the community, a particular person or group, or an idea. Your own self-esteem or self-respect is an important aspect of being able to respect other things.

Young people can show compassion for others by helping them and being their friends.

A sense of justice

Treating everyone fairly is the basis of justice. Working towards a fairer world is one of the main purposes of global citizenship. If more people take on the responsibilities of being active global citizens, then the world can become a fairer place for all of the world's people to live in.

A sense of responsibility

The values of honesty, compassion, respect, and a sense of justice help people behave responsibly to others and their community. Responsibility is one of the duties of being a good citizen.

Courage

It takes personal courage to stand up for ideas and to act on them. Courage helps you do the right thing even when it is not popular. You do not have to be a famous hero to show courage. People can be everyday heroes through their actions and leadership.

justice
fairness and equality

courage
to be able to face and deal with fear, pain, or danger

Young people can show courage and leadership by standing up for the values they believe in.

Peaceful solutions

Some problems are very difficult to solve. This sometimes causes tension and conflict. Active citizens try to solve problems in peaceful ways rather than using force or arguing violently.

conflict
violent disagreement

Thinking deeply

Active citizens need to be able to think deeply about issues. Someone who can do this is called a critical thinker.

To become an active critical thinker you could:

◎ read a range of different books, newspapers, and other print matter
◎ use the Internet to do more research
◎ watch TV news, current affairs programs, and documentaries
◎ listen to others
◎ participate in classroom discussions.

issues
problems or questions that need to be settled

critical thinker
a person who thinks deeply about issues and different points of view to arrive at their own opinion

How do you practice critical thinking?

Critical thinking is a process. It is a series of steps that you go through before you arrive at an opinion.

In many news reports, the Philippines is presented as a place of poor housing and living conditions.

Checklist for critical thinking

✔ Be curious.
✔ Check facts carefully.
✔ Be able to give reasons for your decision.
✔ Consider the consequences of your decision.
✔ Check your own ideas.
✔ Write and express your ideas clearly.
✔ Ask yourself: were you right?

Critical thinking leads to action

Critical thinking helps you arrive at your own opinion. It helps you form ideas about issues. A critical thinker makes choices between different solutions to a problem or question. You can then decide if you want to take action as a result.

The media influences thinking

media
the ways in which information is spread

The media is a very powerful tool. Millions of people around the world use different forms of media every day. The media spreads information in a number of ways:

◎ TV and radio
◎ newspapers, magazines, and books
◎ advertising brochures, signs, and billboards
◎ the Internet and CD-ROMs.

The way things are presented in the media can affect the way people think about an issue, a person, a place, or an event. Sometimes, the news on TV and in the paper only gives a troubled view of the world. There could be trouble in these places, but there are also many good and happy things happening in them. When travel brochures show places looking beautiful to attract tourists, they are trying to influence people's thinking in another way.

A critical thinker collects a range of information. Then, they think deeply about the different viewpoints before arriving at their own opinion.

Travel brochures show part of the Philippines as a beautiful place that tourists would like to visit. This contrasts with pictures of poverty that may be seen on news reports. Which view is correct?

What can I do?
I'm going to start to think more deeply about things. Before I make my mind up about an issue, I'm going to read about it, and watch different TV news programs. I'll discuss it with my mom, too. She's real smart!

What is the global system?

The global system is made up of many different things happening at the same time. They mix with one another. They affect each other. We are all part of this global system, which is made up of:

◎ **The environment**—Many different environments cover the globe. They can be part of the natural environment or the built environment. Natural environments include living things, landforms, soil, air, and water. Built environments include roads, towns, cities, farms, dams, factories, and monuments.

◎ **Society and culture**—Societies are people living together in groups. They develop a culture or way of life that suits them. Culture is passed down from generation to generation. The globe contains many different societies and cultures.

◎ **Heritage**—Many parts of a culture and the natural environment survive over a long time. They become part of the world's heritage. Heritage is passed down through history to the next generation.

◎ **Connecting links**—The globe is a dynamic place where links connect people every day. We can easily communicate from country to country by phone or the Internet. We can see on TV what is happening around the world. We can buy products from different countries.

natural environment
the surroundings that are part of nature

built environment
the surroundings that have been made or built by people

culture
the beliefs, values, and customs of a particular group of people

The global system is a complex web of forces happening at the same time.

Environments

Society and culture

Heritage

Connections

Our global commons

To have something in common with someone means that you share something with them. You might share things like a hobby, a sporting interest, being crazy about the same pop star, or caring about nature.

As global citizens we all have some things in common. These are our global commons:

◎ Air is a global common because it surrounds Earth, we all breathe it, and it cannot be owned.

◎ Water is a global common because most places on Earth have rain and rivers that people can share to provide freshwater for drinking, cooking, and personal hygiene.

◎ Oceans cover nearly 70 percent of Earth's surface. They are not owned by any countries, and can be shared.

◎ Polar lands are a global common in a similar way to oceans.

◎ Human rights are a global common because all people share the claim to have a good life.

global commons
the things that all people on Earth share and that are not owned by anyone

human rights
the basic claims that all people have to fair, safe, and comfortable lives

All people have the right to share in the world's global commons.

What is a global issue?

A global issue is a problem or question that many of the world's citizens are concerned about. There are many global issues facing the world today in both the natural and human environments.

GLOBAL FACT

Tigers are killed for products that can be sold illegally. Tiger bones are valued as medicine and their skins are used as trophies.

Global environments
Our surroundings are where people, plants, animals, and other creatures live. Global citizens protect what we have and limit the amount of damage to our environments.

Human rights
All humans have the right to a fair, safe, and comfortable life. Global citizens try to understand what human rights are so that they can protect them.

Cultural differences
There are many different societies and cultures in the world. Global citizens learn to live with one another by showing respect for these differences.

Quality of life

Many people in the world do not have the same opportunities as others because of poverty. Global citizens try to improve the quality of these people's lives.

Sustainable living

All people use the world's natural resources. Global citizens develop everyday living practices that help limit the effect that people have on Earth.

World heritage

Global citizens want to protect important natural and built features so that they last for future generations.

Global connections

The countries and peoples of the world are now linked very closely through computers, communications equipment, business, and international aid organizations.

Protecting global environments

The natural environment is made up of different ecosystems. Each ecosystem has features that set it apart from others. Four of the world's main ecosystems are tropical rain forests, mountains, coasts, and polar lands. Each has issues related to it.

ecosystems
the relationships between a group of living things in their environment

fragile
easily damaged or destroyed

pristine
totally unspoiled by humans

Ecosystem	Issue of concern
Tropical rain forests	Rain forest trees help produce the oxygen in the air we breathe. Rain forest areas are being logged for timber and cleared for human settlement.
Mountain areas	Most mountain plants are rare and fragile. More and more people are visiting mountain areas as tourists and tramping over plants.
Coasts	Many people enjoy beautiful coastal scenery. There are more and more high-rise apartments being built too close to the sea, blocking views and changing the nature of the shoreline.
Polar lands	The ice regions of Antarctica and the Arctic are the last pristine environments left in the world. Scientific exploration and tourism are increasing and spoiling these polar lands.

Scientific research is important but it has resulted in a lot of waste being dumped in Antarctica.

What can I do?

I'm going to join some of the other kids in my neighborhood to help clean up the local stream on World Environment Day on June 5.

Living sustainably

Everyday living causes pressures on Earth's natural resources. People use resources to feed and clothe themselves, to build houses and workplaces, to generate power, and to make other things. However, we cannot keep using resources at the rate we are today. Resources will run out if we do. To help prevent this, we can:

◎   use fewer resources in our everyday lives
◎   put back or renew some of the resources
◎   avoid spoiling natural resources.

If we practice these habits, we will live in a more sustainable way than we do now. The world can work towards ecologically sustainable development.

natural resources
things that occur naturally, which humans can use

ecologically sustainable development
living in a way that reduces human impact on Earth and helps preserve resources for the future

Coal is a natural resource used to make electricity. This resource will run out because people are using more electricity every day.

Growing organic vegetables and fruit in a community garden plot or in the backyard is a sustainable living practice.

What can I do?

There's a piece of city land not being used for anything in my neighborhood. Some friends and I are putting together a petition to ask the city government if we can use it as a community garden plot.

Respecting others

The world's people come from about 195 different countries and places within these countries. People can be different from each other because of their:

◎ racial origins (also known as ethnicity)
◎ religious beliefs
◎ languages
◎ family structures
◎ ability levels
◎ appearances
◎ cultural traditions
◎ systems of government
◎ levels of wealth.

racial
belonging to a group of people with the same beginnings and physical features

ethnicity
belonging to the same race

Diversity is important

The world's people share the same planet. They have many things in common, but there are also differences between them. If people are to get along together, it is important to value and respect others. The differences between people give the world a rich diversity of life. Diversity is essential in helping the world be a fairer and better place for all people to live in.

Learning to respect people, despite their differences, is an important global issue.

What can I do?

There are 10 different ethnic groups at my school. I'm going to ask my teacher if one or two students from each group can talk at an assembly. It would be good to hear about their customs, beliefs, and families.

Valuing our world's heritage

One thing most people have in common is that they value something from their past. This might be a favorite toy from their childhood, a special photo, a family treasure handed down from generation to generation, a story that tells of ancient times, or a traditional song.

In the same way, planet Earth contains things of value that are handed down from generation to generation. These could be part of the natural environment or something of cultural value. They are part of our heritage.

People often keep a family treasure in a safe place and care for it. We can care for our world heritage in a similar way. Heritage features that are protected and cared for become a gift from the past to the people of the future.

world heritage
significant features in the natural and cultural environments that need protecting

The giant waterfall area at Victoria Falls between Zambia and Zimbabwe, Africa, is part of the world's natural heritage.

These toas are made of wood, clay, and ocher. They are connected to a particular Australian-Aboriginal site and are part of Australia's cultural heritage.

What can I do?
The heritage of my people in Australia stretches back more than 60,000 years. I value my cultural heritage. I'd like to share it with other kids. I'll start a Web page to connect to lots of kids and share my heritage.

Understanding human rights

Most of us know what our rights are in the society we live in. However, we also need to think about whether the rights we have are shared by all people in the world.

In the world's democracies, human rights are based on:

◎ freedom
◎ a level of wealth that buys basic comforts
◎ protection from harm and conflict.

Where any of these are missing, human rights are at risk.

Human rights at risk in the world

There are many cases in the world where people are not treated fairly. Their human rights are at risk in these situations:

◎ Children who live in poor countries are often forced to work from an early age for very little money. Most children in other countries are going to school and getting an education.

◎ Young people who live in war-torn countries are often left without parents and homes. They are forced to run away to look for a better place to live, but are often not welcome in the new places.

◎ People living in countries that do not allow freedom of speech cannot discuss their opinions openly.

◎ Some countries do not allow people to vote to elect the members of their government.

These young people's human rights have been spoiled by war. They have been left homeless.

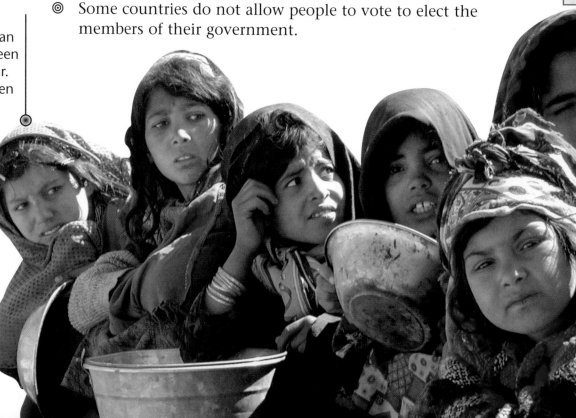

26

Improving the quality of life

GLOBAL FACT

GLOBAL FACT

One out of every four people in the world has a very poor standard of living.

Many people need help to improve their quality of life. The quality of life is the day-to-day living conditions or the standard of living. These things are part of people's standard of living:

◎ Do people have a sufficient amount of nutritious food?

◎ Is there enough clean water?

◎ Do people have comfortable homes to live in?

◎ Do they have TV, radio, newspapers, a phone, and a computer?

◎ Is there proper sanitation and garbage collection in the local area?

◎ Is everyone under the age of 15 able to attend school?

◎ Do the children in a community have the time and places to play and relax?

If we look around, we can sometimes find people within our own community whose quality of life is lower than normal. Street kids and homeless old people are examples. Even within wealthy countries, such as the U.S., the United Kingdom, and Australia, there are people whose quality of life needs to be improved.

standard of living
everyday living conditions in a community

sanitation
clean and safe removal of human and household waste by water and drains

This child is not receiving enough nutritious food and has a poor quality of life.

Even in wealthy countries such as the U.S. there are people whose lives could be better. Groups such as the Salvation Army provide some help.

27

Links around the globe

Our globe is becoming a smaller place. Today, there are many different ways people are linked together across the world. This is known as globalization.

Some people think about globalization in terms of large fast-food, entertainment, and motor-vehicle companies. These global connections are part of the business world. There are also other ways that people can make global connections. The use of computers and the Internet has helped make these global connections even faster.

globalization
the effect of making the world smaller through global connections

Sister schools connect students globally

There is an international movement of sister schools where a school in one country or state has close links with at least one other school in another region. These close links help students develop a deeper understanding of another culture and language. The sister schools program is a way to explore differences. Students also discover what similarities exist between their lives.

Exchange students make global connections

Students can also connect to different parts of the world through exchange programs. These allow students from one country to go and live in another country for several months or more. The students live with a family, go to school, and become part of the everyday culture of the country. Many take part in activities such as working in fields close to the home of their "adopted" family.

Stewart Collins worked in the fields of the village he lived in as an exchange student in northern Thailand.

Sister cities are connected globally

Local communities can connect to communities in a similar way to sister schools. They become sister cities. The government officials of the two communities make an agreement to connect.

The sister city partnership means that the two communities have a friendly link. They exchange information. Sister city programs involve the three main parts of a community, which are local government, businesses, and a wide variety of citizens.

Tourism connects people globally

One of the world's major activities is tourism. People all over the world travel as tourists for three main reasons:
◎ to visit relatives
◎ for recreation and interest
◎ for business.
When people become tourists they travel outside their own community. They make links with different ways of living in the places they visit.

Aid connects people globally

Rich countries help poorer countries through foreign aid programs. Sometimes foreign aid is given in the form of money from one government to another. Other programs give assistance in the form of workers or education to help improve the living conditions. In times of disaster, the aid is in the form of emergency assistance, such as food and medical supplies. Foreign aid from richer countries to poorer ones is a global connection.

GLOBAL FACT

It is expected that by 2010 more than 900 million people will be tourists every year.

foreign aid
help from one country to another by giving money or assistance

World Vision is an organization that sends helpers to countries that need foreign aid.

Being active citizens

We are all citizens of the world. Some of us are more active than others. We become active citizens when we put our ideas into action. Some people think that "action" means protesting or doing something violent. But action can take many forms and can always be peaceful, even in a protest march.

These are some actions that can help make a difference:
◎ keep informed about events and tell others
◎ think deeply about issues
◎ volunteer and take part in community activities
◎ help out wherever you can
◎ stand up for others
◎ join groups that care about the environment and people
◎ use less and make less waste in your day-to-day life
◎ reuse and recycle.

Active global citizens can make a difference in the quality of global environments and the well-being of all people. Remember: an idea is only an idea until someone puts it into action.

What can we do?
Global citizens discuss global issues to try to find ways of solving them. There is hope for the planet if global citizens act together.

Glossary

action something that a person does and the way they do it

adoption to take someone else's child legally into a new family

built environment the surroundings that have been made or built by people

citizen a person living in a larger group of people who they mix with

conflict violent disagreement

courage to be able to face and deal with fear, pain, or danger

critical thinker a person who thinks deeply about issues and different points of view to arrive at their own opinion

culture the beliefs, values, and customs of a particular group of people

customs the usual ways of doing things

democracies countries where the government is freely elected by all the people

diversity the range of different things

ecologically sustainable development living in a way that reduces human impact on Earth and helps preserve resources for the future

ecosystems the relationships between a group of living things in their environment

elect to choose someone for a position by voting

environments natural and built surroundings

ethnicity belonging to the same race

exploit to use selfishly and for personal gain

foreign aid help from one country to another by giving money or assistance

fostering to care for someone else's child within a different family

fragile easily damaged or destroyed

freedom not being controlled by others

global commons the things that all people on Earth share and that are not owned by anyone

globalization the effect of making the world smaller through global connections

human rights the basic claims that all people have to fair, safe, and comfortable lives

ideals something to aim for

identity a person's own character

issues problems or questions that need to be settled

justice fairness and equality

media the ways in which information is spread

nation a large number of people living in a country under the same government

natural environment the surroundings that are part of nature

natural resources things that occur naturally, which humans can use

peer group friends and others you mix with of about the same age

pristine totally unspoiled by humans

racial belonging to a group of people with the same beginnings and physical features

respect a high opinion of someone or something

responsibilities duties that have to be done

rights fair claims to things in daily life

sanitation clean and safe removal of human and household waste by water and drains

self-esteem the opinion you have of yourself

standard of living everyday living conditions in a community

values the ideas and behavior that a group wants its members to follow

wealth the amount of money and resources that a person or country has

well-being the situation of being happy, healthy, and comfortable

world heritage significant features in the natural and cultural environments that need protecting

Index

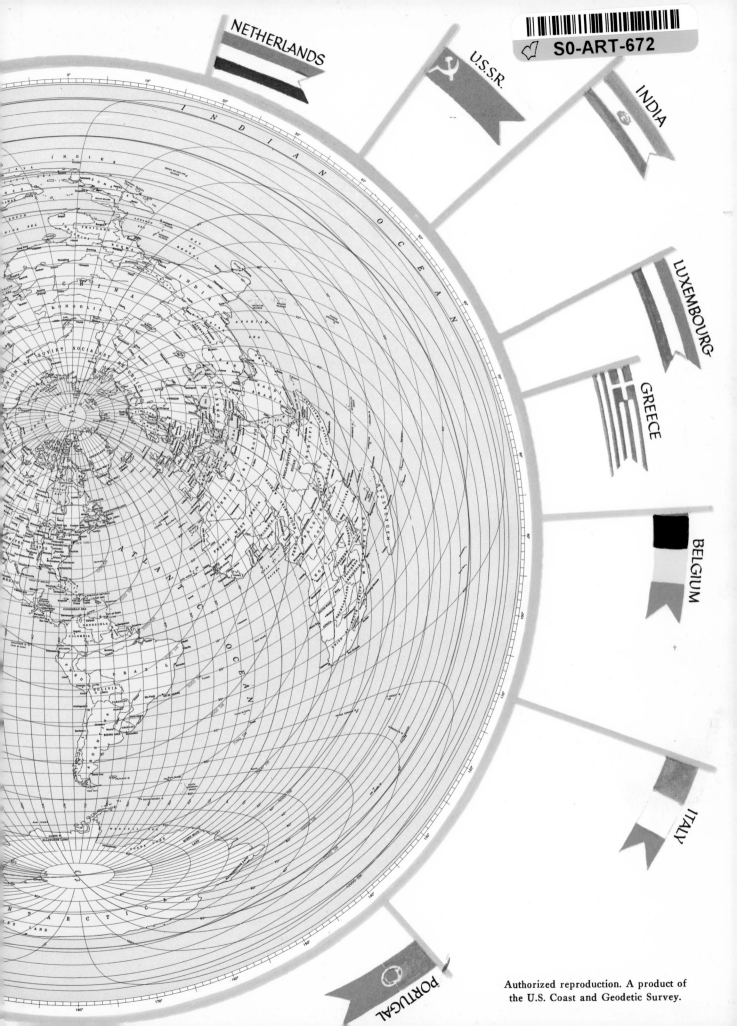

NETHERLANDS

U.S.S.R.

INDIA

LUXEMBOURG

GREECE

BELGIUM

ITALY

PORTUGAL

Authorized reproduction. A product of
the U.S. Coast and Geodetic Survey.

Children

W —

To Abbie and her father

Around the World

N

E

S

by *Miriam Troop*

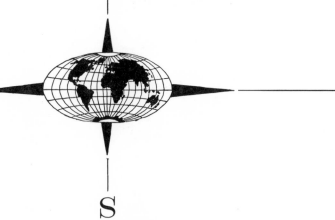

ISBN 0-448-02877-8 (Trade Edition)
ISBN 0-448-03373-9 (Library Edition)

GROSSET & DUNLAP · Publishers · NEW YORK

1971 PRINTING

GREAT BRITAIN 8

KOREA 34

IRELAND 66

JAPAN 14

AUSTRIA 38

CUBA 70

HOLLAND 18

ITALY 42

RUSSIA 74

MEXICO 22

GERMANY 48

GREECE 78

SWITZERLAND 26

INDIA 52

NORWAY 82

CANADA 30

ISRAEL 58

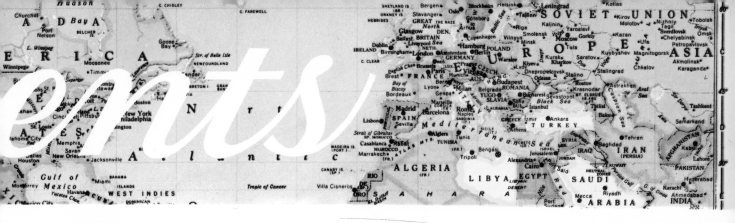

INTRODUCTION

One summer day in France, as I was making my farewell to all of Paris before leaving for New York and home, a letter arrived. "Could you stay a bit longer and bring back sketches and notes about European children?" It was signed Kirk Wilkinson, Art Editor of *Woman's Day*. These lines sent me off on new trips and resulted in pages filled with drawings of children and comments about them and about their countries. Months later I came back with enough material not only for *Woman's Day* magazine, but for other writing and drawing assignments as well.

Several chapters in this book are the result of that first trip. Other material was gathered during later assignments. The sketches of Japanese and Korean children were done during a trip to the Far East for the U.S. Army. Canada and Mexico were visited during vacation trips.

Some day there may be another book which will include the many countries you don't find among the group here. Until that time these represent as much variety and color as I could gather from my notes.

Several people helped me put this book together. Many thanks to them. My deepest gratitude, however, must go to the children whose faces you will see recorded in the pages of this book.

They posed for me patiently, answered questions carefully and guided me through their towns with pride. Best of all, they left me with the precious knowledge that trust, wonder, curiosity and kindness belong to no one nationality, but live in the hearts of boys and girls everywhere.

Miriam Troop

Great Britain

Of all the countries in the world you could visit, Great Britain is the one most like the United States. Imagine finding everyone in a foreign land speaking the same language you speak at home. Understanding their language so well is one good reason why it is easy to make friends with strangers there, and if you were in England, you might very well meet someone just like nine-year-old Derek George Charles Oliver Scott.

Derek lives in Richmond, a tree-lined suburb of one of the largest cities in the world. That city is London and it has over 8,000,000 people. If you were to fly low over London in an airplane, you would see the very old Tower Bridge which crosses the river Thames in the

View of Tower Bridge
from the Tower of London

heart of the old part of the city. Big steamers and freighters sail the forty miles of river from the open sea right up to the center of London. Then, when they get to the bridge, automobile traffic is halted and the bridge is raised, allowing the big ships to pass. The Thames is one of the busiest rivers in the world, and its banks are lined with wharves and docks for miles. The river itself is 209 miles long.

On one side of the river is one of England's most historic spots, the Tower of London, which was built almost 900 years ago in the time of William the Conqueror. In fact, there are even traces of a more ancient wall within the Tower of London. It was built by the Romans to guard the city which they had named Londinium. Many years ago the royal family lived in the central part of the structure, called the White Tower. The other part of the building was a prison. Today, however, the Tower is a quiet museum. It is guarded by the Yeomen of the Guard, or Beefeaters, as they are usually called. In the days of the Tudors these guards also served as waiters. It was a period when beef was eaten on a grand scale and this fact, many

Derek Scott

people believe, resulted in the popular name of Beefeaters. The men wear black velvet hats, scarlet and gold coats, and carry tasseled halberds. A halberd is both a spear and a battle-ax and was used in warfare over 300 years ago.

After a long tour of London, Derek would probably suggest that you join him for a "spot of tea." It is a national custom in Great Britain to stop work at four o'clock and have a cup of tea or milk and perhaps a cookie or sandwich.

Derek's red cap and blazer and the handsome red- and gray-striped tie mean that he goes to a public school. There, all boys wear the same kind of outfit. It is interesting to note that what Americans call

a "private" school, the British call a "public" school. In England public schools such as ours are called elementary schools.

Derek will tell you that after school he likes to play cricket, which he thinks is a little like our game of baseball. But sometimes a cricket match may go on for as long as six days because a player stays at bat until he is put out. Some great batsmen may score more than one hundred runs in one turn at bat! In the meantime there are other interesting things to see in London and, as soon as teatime is over, Derek will suggest a ride on a big red double-decker bus to Piccadilly Circus.

At first it's something of a surprise to discover that the bus is chugging down the "wrong" side of the street. In England, however, all the cars and buses are driven on the left side of the road.

When you get to Piccadilly Circus — where London's famous flower girls sell their blossoms — you will see that it is not a circus at all. It is an open square, much like Times Square in New York City, and Londoners claim it is the very center of the British Empire. Near Piccadilly Circus are Kensington Gardens and Hyde Park where strollers go to watch the ducks and admire the flowers, or to listen to soap-box speeches. Flocks of sheep even graze on the grass there, which is one way of feeding sheep — and keeping the grass trimmed, too! Derek will probably make a point of taking you to one corner of Kensington Gardens to see the statue of Peter Pan.

Next morning at eleven o'clock would be the time to go to Buckingham Palace to watch the ceremonial "Changing of the Guard." The line of mounted Grenadier Guards, in scarlet tunics, blue trousers and black bearskin caps with white goat's hair plumes, makes an impressive sight. If the Queen's personal flag, the Royal Standard, is hoisted on top of the palace, everyone then knows that Queen Elizabeth II is at home. If the flag is not up, the Queen is away, perhaps at Windsor Castle, or on a visit to Scotland with her husband, Prince Philip — the Duke of Edinburgh — and their children, Prince Charles, Princess Anne, Prince Andrew and Prince Edward.

Everybody on a visit to London wants to see Westminster Abbey,

Derek buys flowers for his mother
from a Piccadilly flower girl

St. Paul's Cathedral at the head of Ludgate Hill

where the Queen and most English monarchs since William the Conqueror have been crowned. It holds the tombs of many famous men. Only a short walk from the Abbey are the magnificent Houses of Parliament where the House of Commons and the House of Lords meet. Above Parliament rises a high tower in which the famous clock, Big Ben, bongs out the hours.

But Derek doesn't spend all his time in London. For a summer vacation his parents may take him to the seashore — perhaps to Cornwall in southern England or to Brighton, a seaside resort.

Last summer Derek visited Oxford and Cambridge, where the two world-famous universities of the same names are located. He still hasn't decided which one he would like to attend. Once he went to visit his grandmother in Scotland. He traveled through small country villages notable for their thatched-roof cottages and hedges of primroses and hollyhocks. He drove through Liverpool, England's second largest port city, and through the great coal-mining center near Newcastle. In Glasgow, a kilted Scotsman taught Derek how to play the bagpipes.

For a shilling, you can look across the Thames from Richmond to London

Beefeaters at the Tower of London

It may come as a surprise to you to learn that the British Isles are smaller than the state of New Mexico! But rarely has a small country had such an illustrious history and such a great empire. In fact, our history is more closely linked to Great Britain's than to that of any other country. Our form of government, some of the ways in which we worship, our language and many of our democratic institutions have all been inherited from Great Britain.

Hiroshi in Ueno Park, Tokyo
where cherry blossoms grow

Japan

You would probably never guess that this young boy walking through the park is a well-known Japanese actor with four years of stage experience. His name is Hiroshi Terajima and he is eleven years old. His father, grandfather and great-great-grandfathers as far back as eight generations have all been actors. But in many ways he is just like any American boy. For instance, he has a special interest in baseball and Hiroshi is one of the most ardent fans the Tokyo Giants have in all Japan. His curiosity about American baseball teams is enough to make him forget

14

his shyness and invite you to walk along with him as he heads for the famous Tokyo Kabuki Theater in the center of the city.

Breakfast with Mother

Kabuki is the name of a special kind of entertainment and has been very popular with the Japanese ever since the seventeenth century. Kabuki dramas are wonderful folk tales acted with singing and dancing. Traditionally, all the roles are played by men, including women character parts. The actors wear elaborate, colorful costumes and exaggerated make-up. Hiroshi gives two performances a day. If you wait with him in his dressing room before he goes on stage, he will tell you about some interesting Japanese customs.

"Zori" off, shoes on, for walking to school

Before entering a house in Japan, everyone leaves his shoes at the front door and slips into soft scuffs called "zori." Although chairs are found in many Japanese homes today, Hiroshi will tell you that he and his family have none. They prefer to sit on small flat pillows with their toes tucked under them, or directly on the matted floor which is made up of large, thick sectional straw mats called "tatami," placed together like linoleum tiles.

Attendants help to dress Hiroshi

Tea, Japan's popular drink, is served without spoons, sugar, cream or lemon. Many solid foods are eaten with the aid of two short sticks which we call chopsticks. This word is similar to the Chinese word from which it comes, meaning "hasteners" or "speedy ones." The Japanese are very polite — so much so that their manners may seem strange to you at first. Often, they end each sentence of greeting with a deep bow,

Hiroshi learns the fine art of make-up from his father

A modern rickshaw on wheels, called a pedi-cab

and two people bobbing at each other are really only saying "hello."

You will probably want to remember this later when Hiroshi invites you to his home to meet his mother, father and sisters. You will certainly find their small landscaped garden lovely and, if you like, you may peek into the tiny teahouse which some wealthy families build to serve as a special place for tea ceremonies.

As soon as Hiroshi's father comes home from the theater, he replaces his business suit with a soft, silk kimono. His mother is accustomed to the Japanese kimonos so that she never wears clothes like your mother's. His sisters, however, often prefer skirts and blouses, and Hiroshi himself wears shirts and trousers just like those worn by boys in the United States.

Japan consists of a tiny group of islands. Every inch of fertile space has been cultivated carefully so that rice paddies and tilled patches of soil abound everywhere. From the northernmost island of Hokkaido to the southernmost tip of Kyushu there are lakes, waterfalls, mountains, forests, hot springs, geysers and beaches. There are places in the ocean around Japan where pearls are cultivated and Japanese women may be seen diving to the very bottom of the water to gather them. These women are excellent swimmers.

There are cities in Japan dating from ancient times. Kyoto, the capital of Japan from the eighth to the nineteenth centuries, still has the old streets and magnificent shrines that have made it world-famous as a tourist stop. But there

The colors of the kimonos suggest the wearers' ages — bright for young girls, gray and black for matrons

are other cities that have become as modern as ours. In Tokyo, the capital of Japan, the street traffic is quite heavy and there are big department stores where you can buy anything from cricket cages and baseball bats to television sets.

You may have heard of judo, also known as jujitsu. Hiroshi will tell you that its origins go back to the seventeenth century. People all over the world, especially soldiers, study and practice this ancient method of self-defense, which was imported from China.

The enthusiasm of the Japanese for holidays is hard to match. There is one in some part of the country almost every day. In March there is the Doll Festival. In April there is the Flower Festival to commemorate the birthday of Buddha. April is also the month of the Cherry Blossom season and an occasion for much dancing in the streets. But Hiroshi's favorite holiday is the Festival of the Boys which is held each May. This national holiday is also known as Children's Day. Hiroshi likes it best because he often receives gifts.

Japan has been called the most Westernized country of the East. It is hard to believe that only about one hundred years ago, in 1853, Commodore Perry sailed his fleet of ships into Tokyo Bay and opened Japan for the first time to trade with the rest of the world.

A sketch of the Great Buddha of Kamakura — the bronze giant Daibutsú

Holland

Here and there, in tiny corners of the world, you can still find people wearing clothes that look just like those once worn by their grandparents and great-grandparents. They may ride bicycles or listen to the radio or drive new automobiles, but the clothing they put on each morning and the shoes they take off each night have not changed a button in style for hundreds of years.

One such place is Volendam, Holland. This small fishing village, north of Amsterdam, is situated on the shores of the Zuider Zee, which is a lake enclosed by a dike. Everywhere there are men, women and children dressed in black woolen clothes. Women and girls also wear starched, white peaked caps and gay striped aprons — and everybody wears yellow wooden shoes. Many tourists come to see the people of Volendam, not only for a glimpse of their picturesque clothing and quaint buildings, but because of the friendliness and hospitality for which they are also noted. The citizens of Volendam are used to answering questions about themselves, and the children, who ride bicycles wearing their wooden shoes, enjoy showing off.

Ten-year-old Grietje Lindeboom, who lives in Volendam, likes to practice the English she learned in school, and she will understand most questions put to her. But if you asked to

18

see where that famous Dutch boy put his finger in the hole in the dike to save the city, she would only laugh. It is only a story made popular by the book "Hans Brinker or the Silver Skates." Actually, the dike here is six feet thick.

The Netherlands, as Holland is also known to the rest of the world, means "lowlands," and Grietje will tell you that almost a quarter of her country is below sea level. The Dutch have built dikes higher than the sea and have drained off the water and salt to make the land fit for the cultivation of many products, including wheat, potatoes and flax. Much of the Zuider Zee, which was once a part of the North Sea, has been reclaimed

Grietje stands on the high dike that keeps the waters of the Zuider Zee from the homes of Volendam

Grietje's baby brother sleeps in the little compartment below his parents' bed

in this fashion. These areas are called polders and are also the sites of many beautiful tulip beds for which Holland is world-famous.

Before long you will pass the wooden house where Grietje lives. Her mother will probably be outside, especially if it is Friday, scrubbing the walls and polishing the doorbell. Everyone in Holland cleans house on Friday. The tiny house where Grietje lives consists of one big room with a tile fireplace that is used for both cooking and heating. In a corner is an alcove where her parents sleep. Below their bed is a small closet-like compartment where Grietje's baby brother sleeps. Greitje's bed is in another corner.

It is warm and cozy in the house and you will probably be treated to a cup of milk and some bread and cheese. Dutch cheese is delicious and it is exported to countries all over the world. Then, as a special treat, you will be urged to fill your pockets with licorice, shaped like little cats, to take home.

Grietje loves her little village, but she has also traveled to other parts of Holland with her family. She will tell you about the exciting day at The Hague on the third Tuesday in September. There she saw

20

Queen Juliana drive by in a golden coach drawn by six white horses, to open Parliament. The Queen was accompanied by her husband Prince Bernhard and the royal princesses, Beatrix Wilhelmina Armgard, Irene Emma Elisabeth, Margriet Francisca and Maria Christina.

Grietje will tell you about the afternoon she visited the house in Amsterdam where the famous artist Rembrandt lived and painted. Amsterdam is a special place for fun and sight-seeing. It is a city of canals and bridges, making possible a round trip all through Amsterdam by boat. After the ride you may want to visit the royal palace and watch the Punch and Judy show which is given in a little theater on wheels just under the palace windows.

Grietje has also visited Delft, an ancient town famous the world over for its pottery. She will tell you about Leiden, Rembrandt's birthplace, and the scene of Dutch resistance to Spanish invaders. The famous University of Leiden is located here. Then, most surprising of all, Grietje will tell you about our own Pilgrim Fathers. After they left England, they stayed in Amsterdam for a short while. They then went to Leiden and remained in that Dutch city for eleven years before sailing to America on the historic Mayflower.

In Volendam, even dolls wear traditional clothes

Delicious herring is sold and eaten here

A drawbridge, one of many in Holland

Mexico

In Mexico there is a little town which is almost a duplicate of a Spanish town. The Spaniards who came to the New World about 400 years ago to hunt for silver built this town, and it is called Guanajuato. They made it just as they remembered Granada, the town in Spain they had left. The silver mines they discovered and worked made them very rich and they lavished their wealth on homes, churches and other buildings. Their town, high in the mountains, prospered.

But times changed. Mexico had many revolutions and wars. The mines were flooded, the Spaniards left and the town went to sleep. Today, it is no longer rich in mineral wealth, but in appearance and custom it is much the same as it was in former days. Old-fashioned lamps light its streets and beautiful old buildings. Soft guitars can often be heard in the background. Now, in the hills above the town are small pottery factories. They employ many of the men who live in the town below.

You will find young boys working here as apprentices and among them is ten-year-old Pepe Rivera. Pepe goes to school during the day and, because he wants to be a master potter when he grows up, he devotes many hours after school helping to make pots, bowls, vases and urns out of clay.

A modern school for Pepe

Scrambling after Pepe as he shows you his town, you will probably have to stop many times to catch your breath, for Guanajuato is over 6,000 feet high, or more than a mile above sea level. Mexico is a mountainous country split by great canyons and broad, uneven valleys. Hot lowlands are often within view of snow-covered peaks. Pepe will tell you that his Indian ancestors, who lived in these hills centuries ago, named the town Guanajuato, after the croaking sound of frogs they worshiped as gods.

The soft sound of pat-a-pat will stop you as you pass open doorways. Pepe will explain that women are slapping corn dough

Pepe carries a tray of clay pots, ready for the kiln

with their hands to shape it into bread. Later, he will give you some of this bread— a soft, flat pancake called a tortilla. Since it is flat, you will discover that you can use it as a plate for other foods.

Pepe is very fond of history, especially the history of his own country. In 1810, he will tell you proudly, the first bell for freedom was rung in the War of Independence with Spain. The brave priest, Miguel Hidalgo y Costilla, who was born near Guanajuato, issued a now famous declaration calling for liberty. He was later captured by Spanish troops and shot. For his leadership and courageous efforts to free Mexico from Spanish rule, he is often called the George Washington of his country.

Today, of course, Mexico is no longer ruled by Spain. The country is a democracy and elects its presidents as we do. It is the nearest neighbor of the United States to the south. The stormy history of Mexico also has in it bold and ruthless men, many of whom were beloved by the Indians. Two of the more famous were Francisco "Pancho" Villa and Emiliano Zapata.

Pepe will show you a house on a hill where the artist Diego Rivera was born. He and other Mexican painters have produced paintings which have a special Mexican quality.

Pepe likes to read newspapers to learn what is happening in his country. He can tell you all about Paricutín, one of the newest of the many volcanoes in Mexico. It erupted suddenly in a cornfield in 1943, and Pepe has been reading how it has grown to a height of about 7,451 feet.

But even more exciting than the volcano was the rodeo Pepe's uncle took him to see in Mexico City one Saturday. It was held in the plaza at the foot of the terrace where King Maximilian and Queen Charlotte used to look out over the city. Here the Charros, Mexican cowboys famous for

A sketch of Pepe sitting near the statue of Father Hidalgo, fighter for Mexican freedom

their horsemanship, perform perilous feats like lassoing wild horses and fighting enraged bulls.

Pepe loved fast-growing Mexico City, the capital of his country. He will tell you about the colorful shopping stalls in the market places and about the tall apartment houses, fine parks and new school buildings which have made Mexico City one of the world's most modern cities.

He remembers the evenings spent sitting in the great square, called the Zócalo, which is surrounded by flowering bushes and trees. Every town, city or village in Mexico has at least one such square where girls and boys promenade every evening.

Holidays are wonderful fun in Mexico. There are native dances, rodeos, bullfights, races, cockfights, music playing and elaborate fairs. These take place especially in December, which is a big holiday month. There are firecrackers and lots to eat, and Pepe says that he usually eats too many tortillas, his favorite dish.

25

Switzerland

Tucked away in the mountains of Europe is a small country that has had a violent history. Many years of war came to an end when her divided territories, called cantons, were united into a single nation. You may be surprised to know that this action helped guide our own country's forefathers when they drew up the first constitution of the United States, which united the American colonies.

Today Switzerland is a lovely, peaceful country. People from all over the world come here to see the beauty of the Swiss Alps and in the winter, these mountains attract thousands of skiers to their inviting slopes. High in the mountains, in a village called Les Haudères, a little girl named Monique Chevrier is watching from her window as skiers, far in the distance, make faint tracks in the snow.

Monique is a rosy-cheeked eight-year-old who has lived in Les Haudères all her life. Her father, she tells everyone proudly, is the best shoemaker in all of

Monique is proud of her little
town, and enjoys the grand view
of the Alps in the distance

Switzerland. Like so many Americans, Monique is proud of her
mixed ancestry. Her father is of French descent, and Monique's
mother is of German and Italian origin.

Les Haudères is one of the many villages in this country where
women still wear the kind of embroidered hats and full black skirts
that their grandmothers once wore. Monique likes her hat and dress
and even wears it when she goes to Geneva on a special holiday.
Everyone there wears modern clothes, but because so many other
visiting Swiss are in their traditional dress, Monique's costume is not
considered unusual.

In the summer, Monique can open her shutters and look out at the Alps which are then covered with grass, flowers, and trees. Long ago, perhaps in these very hills, so the story goes, lived William Tell, a legendary Swiss patriot who was sentenced to shoot an apple off his son's head with an arrow. Today, you can see cattle grazing peacefully high up in the hills, where the men and older boys have driven them for the summer. Monique wakes every day to the tinkle of cowbells and, at night, she falls asleep to the same musical tones.

Some of the cows' milk is made into cheese and butter in the tiny huts high on the mountain slopes, and then sold in the nearest town. The Swiss cheese you have tasted is a well-known dairy product, exported widely. Swiss chocolate products are also world-famous.

Monique will tell you that the winters here, though beautiful, are very cold. She knows that her grandfather learned to assemble watches entirely by himself, while snowbound. The Swiss are also fine woodcarvers, and the village of Brienz in the Bernese Oberland of Switzerland has long been called the "Woodcarver's Capital" of the world. Monique is not a woodcarver, she admits sadly. Most of her nights are spent by the warm stove with her

The warm slate corner stove is the best place for studying. Family linens under a flat slab of rock press smooth on top

After church the women stand in the warm sun to chat

brother Pierre and sister Cecile, reading and doing homework.

Monique has visited the larger cities of her country, including Zurich, a busy, manufacturing, German-speaking city and the most populous in Switzerland. Zurich is situated at the foot of the Alps and is an important center of learning. Monique has also been to Geneva, at the western end of Lake Geneva, where French is spoken primarily. This city is the headquarters of the International Red Cross, and was the center of the old League of Nations.

Many Swiss people speak Italian, especially in the canton of Ticino. Thus, French, German and Italian are the three official languages of Switzerland. Romansh, a dialect, is recognized as the fourth national language of the country.

Switzerland is one of the oldest republics in the world and, like the United States, has welcomed people who have been forced to flee their homelands because of intolerance and persecution.

29

Canada

Occupying the great expanse of territory north of the United States — an area of 3,845,774 square miles — is Canada, a country often associated with adventure and discovery. The famous Viking, Leif Ericsson, probably explored Canada's eastern shores about 1,000 years ago. Priests and missionaries who went to live with the Indian tribes also made important explorations. In many ways Canada, an Indian word meaning "village," is still a great unknown land.

Like the United States, Canada is made up of people of many nationalities. It is an independent member nation of the British Commonwealth, and the second largest country in the world. Beautiful lakes, forests, mountains and prairie lands stretch across the country, and in its earth have been found all kinds of riches, including coal, oil and uranium.

Twelve-year-old Dalton Brooks has spent most of his life in a tiny fishing village called Peggy's Cove, in Nova Scotia. Nova Scotia, along with New Brunswick, Prince Edward Island and Newfoundland, form the group of provinces on the Canadian Eastern seaboard. Like many of the early English who settled along the rocky coast, Dalton's family are fishermen. Dalton himself can show you how to catch lobster and row a skiff, and he can often tell you whether it will rain or shine. But if you should ask him, Dalton will tell you that he does not want to be a fisherman. He would prefer to be a uranium prospector and live in the wilds of northern Canada.

Dalton learned a great deal about Canada when he traveled with his aunt, uncle and two cousins during a three-month trip across the country last summer. He considers those months the most exciting he has ever spent.

On their trip, Dalton's uncle told the children it would be fun if all of them pretended that they were blazing a trail such as the one made by Canada's famous explorer and fur trader, Sir Alexander Mackenzie, who made the first over-land trip across North America's wilderness. The explorer traveled on foot with only a shoulder pack, but Dalton and his family rode in a station wagon and, in some places, flew by plane. Although they did not follow

Traps for lobsters line the wharf behind Dalton Brooks

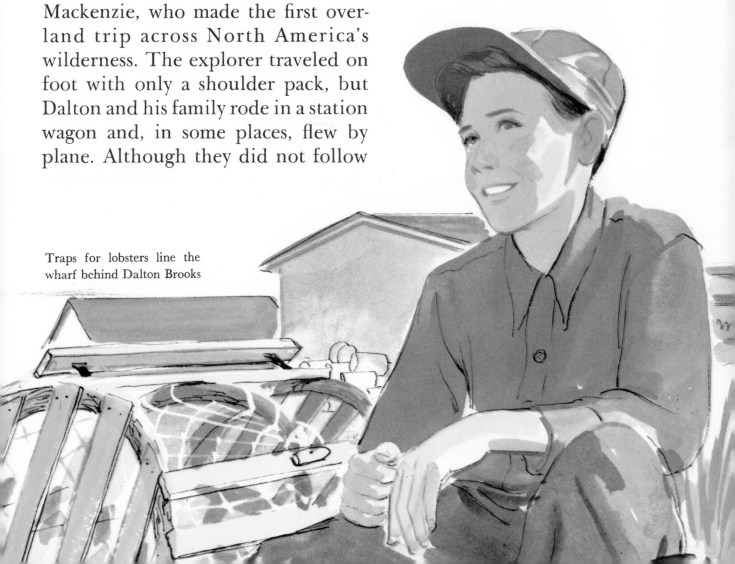

Totem poles of Pacific coast Indians

"Mackenzie's Track," they did cover much of the same territory.

Dalton and his family started out from Montreal, the largest city in Canada, which is on the St. Lawrence River in the province of Quebec. Montreal is one of North America's great ports, and the shipping on the Great Lakes, which lie between Canada and the United States, has helped Montreal grow. Close by is the city of Lachine, at the head of the Lachine Rapids, where Indian canoes once glided across the water.

From Montreal it was not far to Ottawa, the capital city of Canada, which is in the province of Ontario. There Dalton was impressed by the sight of the beautiful Parliament Building and its high clock tower, similar to the clock tower of the British Parliament. Farther south is Toronto, the capital city of the province of Ontario, which was founded on the site of a French fort. The French have played an important role in Canadian history and a large part of its population still speaks French.

Dalton remembers particularly the thrill of visiting Winnipeg, capital of the province of Manitoba. It is situated where the Red and Assiniboine Rivers meet. Here two great Canadian rival fur companies, the Hudson's Bay Company and the North West Company, set up their trading posts. Mighty logs float down the

Maple sugaring time in the eastern province of Quebec

Saskatchewan River which runs into Lake Winnipeg. Then, at Manitoba's largest sawmill, the logs are cut.

In Regina, capital of the province of Saskatchewan, Dalton remembers his visit to the barracks of the Royal Canadian Mounted Police. These are the handsome red-jacketed stalwarts who "always get their man." The "Red Coats" were organized in 1873 to prevent Indian outbreaks. They were few in number then, but today, the "Riders of the Plains" form a larger force and are stationed all over Canada.

Dalton says he will never forget the endless rolling wheat fields in the rich farm country of the province of Alberta. The capital of this province is Edmonton, where thousands of oil wells lined their way.

Many miles away, Dalton, his cousins and aunt and uncle approached the rising foothills that lead to the Canadian Rockies and the westernmost province of British Columbia. Several islands stretch out across the Pacific shore of this mountainous region. The two largest are Queen Charlotte Island and Vancouver.

Some day he hopes to go prospecting for uranium with his Geiger counter up in the Northwest Territories and in the Yukon. The Northwest Territories are, for the most part, thousands of miles of wasteland and the climate is extremely cold. The Yukon is famous for the great gold rush of 1897. When this precious metal was discovered in Klondike Creek thousands of people hurried into the Yukon Territory to join the search for quick riches.

Korea

If you could speak Korean, you would then be able to ask ten-year-old Im Yung-sook and her two best friends why they were wearing their Sunday clothes in the middle of the week. They would tell you that they were celebrating the Korean national Thanksgiving Day. Schools and stores are closed on this holiday and in every house the children have treats of walnuts and apples. Outdoors they play games like Giant Steps, Spider Web or their favorite, which is called "Nul."

This game, similar to teeter-totter or seesaw, is played by two children. Each tries to stay on a board longer and jump higher than the other.

Yung-sook can play this game for hours. Perhaps the little canoe-shaped rubber shoes she wears keep her bouncing. During the week the three friends wear black skirts and white middy blouses, as do all schoolgirls in Korea. They go to the Chong Am primary school on the outskirts of Taegu. There they study drawing, arithmetic, music, dancing, the Korean language and gymnastics.

School is very important to Korean children, for education is held in high regard. The scholars and artists of this "Hermit Kingdom," as it was once called, have enjoyed great honor during its 2,000 years of recorded history. These Korean scholars and artists not only helped in developing their own culture, but also made important contributions to the culture of Japan. But scholarship and art did not prevent Korea's neighbors from attacking her. At various times China or Japan dominated this little land.

In more modern times under Japanese occupation, Chosen, as the

A typical farm terraced with rice fields. Against the grass-roofed huts, red peppers dry in the sun

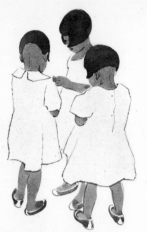

The most popular haircut for
little girls — cut high in back

A Korean grandfather.
His white robe is a
symbol of mourning

American soldiers are seen
often in South Korean cities

Japanese called Korea, became the bridge for new
ideas from China to feudal Japan. The rich rice
fields of Korea helped to supply food for Japan's
overpopulated islands. Later though, and for her
own purposes, Japan helped to speed some phases
of Korea's development.

Once out of the crowded cities, you will find the
lovely Korean countryside terraced with rice fields.
The mountains rise high above the tiny grass-roofed
huts with their clean-swept courtyards. Red peppers
lie drying in the sun and huge earthen crocks line
the walls of the huts. These crocks hold the hot,
odorous pickled preserves used as food flavoring.

In the winter, cold Siberian winds blow fiercely.
During these chilly nights Yung-sook and her family sleep on mattresses and blankets laid directly
on the oil-paper floor. The floor is heated from below by ducts which carry the smoke and heat from
cooking fires. The beds are kept comfortable even
through the coldest winter.

Following World War II, Korea was divided by a
boundary line into two parts, each with a different
form of government. Several years later, North
Korea, with the help of other countries, invaded
South Korea.

It wanted, by force, to control the whole country.
However, the United Nations, led principally by
the United States, came to the aid of the democratic
South Korean government. It was one of the achievements of the United Nations that it helped South
Korea to defend herself and to drive back the aggres-
sors. Later, an armistice was signed by the two sides.

Yung-sook and her family look forward to the
day when North and South Korea will be united
again under a democratic form of government.

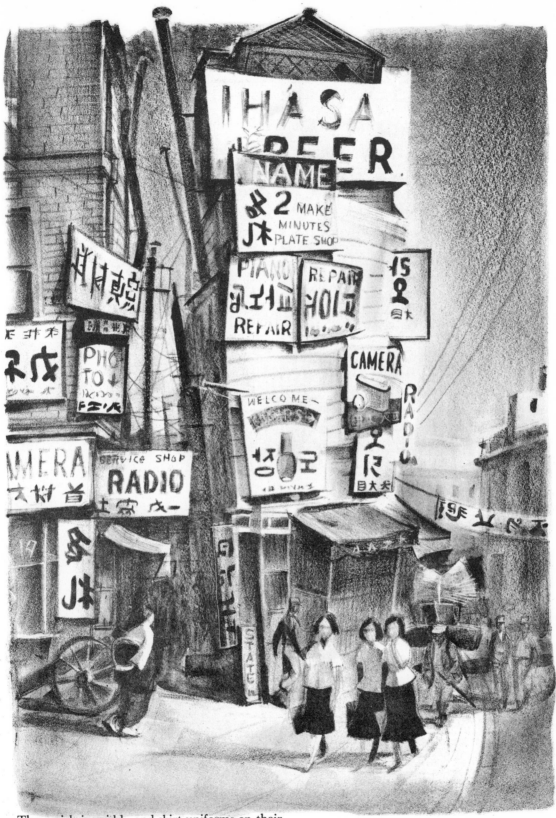

Three girls in middy and skirt uniforms on their
way to school through the busy streets of Taegu

Fritz wears his ski boots to class. During the winter he skis to school and back

Austria

Austria has some of the thickest forests in all of Europe, a fact which may explain why there are so many woodcarvers there. Remember that carved cuckoo clock your grandmother had and those happy painted faces that formed nutcrackers? Well, today you can still find Austrian boys who are longing to be woodcarvers and who report for work at the studio of a master carver every day after school.

One such boy who lives in Innsbruck, the capital of the romantic mountain region of Austria called the Tyrol, is eleven-year-old Fritz Jager. Fritz is a champion skier and a powerful yodeler. He has used his skis each winter since he learned to walk and he is not afraid of the highest ski runs. His yodeling has made him the most envied boy in the mountains of Innsbruck. Herr Reindl, who is teaching Fritz how to carve beautiful things out of wood, says that he is a talented student. The proof is that Fritz can carve out a four-inch angel in a single afternoon.

Fritz will tell you that before World War I, Austria was united with Hungary in the Austro-Hungarian Empire. The two kingdoms had separate parliaments, although both nations were ruled by the Austrian Emperor and acted together in their relations with other countries. After their defeat in the war the Austro-Hungarian Empire was broken up. Austria became a republic in 1918, but Hungary did not last long as a republic and restored the monarchy soon afterward.

Learning the fine art of woodcarving

Fritz skis high in the Austrian Alps

In 1938 Austria let itself be seized by Germany. After Germany's defeat in World War II, Austria was reestablished as a republic.

On the day of independence, Fritz's parents have told him, the country was filled with singing, dancing and loud yodeling. There was much celebrating as Austrians danced the Schuhplattler, the national folk dance, to the rhythm of handclapping. Peasants wearing leather pants and the gay feathers of the heath cock in their hats smoked long curved pipes and yodeled to the sound of zithers. The children were dressed in their native costumes and the women wore lovely Tyrolean dirndls, or embroidered skirts, blouses and colorful aprons.

As a special treat to celebrate the anniversary of the day of independence, Fritz's father recently took him on his first visit to Vienna. It was an exciting ride from the narrow streets and picturesque

40

houses of Innsbruck to the modern capital of Austria. The street traffic was bustling in the capital city and Fritz saw many new buildings and a modern-style railway station in Vienna. He liked especially the rebuilt Vienna state opera house, which some people believe is the most modern in the world.

Fritz will never forget walking along the shores of the Danube River and finding it brown, and not at all blue as it is in song and legend! From the river you can look up to the hills of the Vienna Woods and see the landscape which inspired Beethoven's magnificent Pastoral Symphony. Fritz learned from his father that Vienna was once a Roman citadel. He especially enjoyed his ride on the great ferris wheel at the Prater, Vienna's famous park.

Fritz's father also took him to Salzburg where one of the world's most celebrated music festivals is held each year. High above the city stands an old fortress from whose height Fritz could watch the traffic in the narrow streets far below. Here he listened to a carillon of thirty-five bells ringing melodies from Mozart's immortal music.

They wanted to remain in Salzburg a while longer, but Christmas was coming and there was much to be done. Fritz wanted to finish the carving of a whole set of figures for the Nativity scene. These figures, called a crèche, are brought down from Austrian attics every year and put on view for the holiday. They may be simple or quite elaborate woodcarvings. Most of them portray the Christ child in the manger, Mary, Joseph, the Three Kings, shepherds and the animals of the stable. Many carved sets take a long time to make and some have been preserved for hundreds of years. Fritz thinks his crèche will be the best in Innsbruck.

A spring festival brings out children in costume . . .

and dancers . . .

dancing the Schuhplattler . . .

and colorful musicians

Italy

Just a short distance from the toe of the "boot" that is Italy lies the island of Sicily. Its capital and major port is the quaint and busy city of Palermo. If you are in Palermo from July 13th to the 15th you will have a wonderful treat. These days mark the annual Feast of Santa Rosalia, patron saint of Palermo. As a part of the religious celebration there is a gay Cart Festival.

The people here show a fond affection for their horses and donkeys. Their horses and even the wagons that they use are always gaily decorated, and simple carts are often painted from end to end in brilliant colors. The horses may be wearing hats bedecked with bright red feathers and gold pompons or with fringes of silk tassels and plumes. Silver scrollwork often decorates their polished leather reins. But no matter how elegant the horses may seem all year round it is little compared to the way they are embellished on the day of the Cart Festival, at which time a prize is awarded for the most elaborate horse and cart.

A recent prizewinning cart in gay shades of red, yellow and blue was covered with paintings of saints, cupids and crusader heroes. Twelve-year-old Stefano Rubino was the lucky boy who held the artist's brushes. He was even allowed to paint one of the tiny cupid faces on the right wheel. Stefano is apprenticed to Signor Salve, who paints the gayest carts in all Palermo. During the morning there is school to attend, but afterward Stefano is at the shop, watching and helping the artists paint wagon after wagon.

After ten years of study with Signor Salve, Stefano will have his own shop. Some day, Stefano will tell you, he may even try to paint other things. He knows that in his country there have lived some of the world's greatest painters. Of these, Michelangelo, Raphael and Botticelli are his favorites.

Stefano paints the inside of a wagon

A street where fishermen live on the island of Capri

Stefano will tell you that Italians have always been artistic people. Every Italian city has its own beautiful buildings, monuments and paintings. Rome, the capital, is one of the most beautiful cities in the world. For many years travelers from all over the world have been delighted by the beauty found in its landscapes, its ancient ruins, its works of art, its churches, fountains and buildings. Rome is the birthplace of an ancient civilization which left its mark on a great part of the world. The Vatican, home of the Roman Catholic religion, is here and to it 550 million followers all over the world look for guidance.

Tradition has it that Rome, the "City of Seven Hills," was founded by Romulus more than 2,700 years ago. He and his twin brother Remus, the legend goes, were nourished by a she-wolf who found the abandoned infants in a forest. Slowly the city grew and finally expanded into an empire which conquered many lands. The Roman Empire lasted over four centuries. One of its greatest achievements was a code of law drawn up under Justinian that is the foundation for much of the civil law in some parts of Europe even now.

After having gone through many wars, and a dictatorship, Italy is a free country today. On June 2, 1946, Stefano will tell you, the Italian people voted in favor of a republic. It was a joyous day for Italy and especially in Sicily where gaily decorated horses and bright-colored carts were part of the festivities.

As you walk along the streets of Palermo with Stefano, you can see how densely populated the city is, as is the case for all Italy. For this reason, many Italians have left their country to seek jobs and new opportunities elsewhere. These emigrants brought the Italian love of laughter and song with them wherever they settled. A natural gift for singing has made many of them famous. The La Scala Opera House in Milan is one of the most celebrated opera houses in the world and students come here from many countries to study singing. Milan, the second largest city in Italy, is also an important industrial center.

Stefano can tell you much about other Italian cities, even though he has never left Palermo. He knows about them from his older brother who has been almost everywhere in Italy. Stefano's favorite is museum-filled Florence, the magnificent city of the Renaissance, where old streets, churches and houses date back to the time of the Medicis, a powerful and ruthless ruling family. An ancient covered bridge called the Ponte Vecchio still spans the Arno River in Florence. Once a year you may witness the colorful Calcio here, which coincides with the opening of the University of Florence. It is a traditional football game played by young men wearing historical Florentine costumes.

In the south is Naples, one of the chief seaports in Italy. The city is set among olive and orange trees and faces the lovely Bay of Naples. Nearby is the volcano of Mount Vesuvius which erupted in A.D. 79, destroying the cities of Pompeii, Herculaneum and Stabiae. Recent excavations in these cities have uncovered much about the way of life during that period, because the volcanic ash preserved almost

An ancient house in Florence darkens a narrow street

everything it touched. Mount Vesuvius is still steaming, and it is the only active volcano on the European mainland today.

Stefano will tell you about Venice, "the Queen of the Adriatic," made up of more than one hundred small islands. Hundreds of bridges span the waterways in Venice, and gondolas take the place of streetcars and automobiles. Other important cities are Genoa, the birthplace of Columbus, and Pisa with its famous Leaning Tower. One of the most important centers of learning during the Middle Ages was located in Bologna. The University of Bologna is still in existence.

Most of the people in Italy are farmers, and much of the land is used for grain crops. Many Italians are vegetarians, perhaps because there is little land for grazing animals. Spaghetti with tomato sauce and cheese is a popular dish here. Beans and macaroni are also favorites. A typical grocery store in Italy displays dozens of different shapes and kinds of macaroni and spaghetti, and just as many different cheeses. The cheeses are coated with a protective covering so that they may be kept fresh for long periods. Of course, the large crisp loaves of Italian bread, often covered with sesame seeds, are a part of every meal.

Italy grows fine olives and Stefano's joy in watching his "maestro" work at painting carts is never complete without munching on a pocketful of olives. Indeed, if olives could make one a talented painter, Stefano would probably be the greatest artist the world has ever known.

46

Before leaving Italy, Stefano will introduce you to his uncle, who is a member of the Carabinieri, a proud military police group which was first organized during the days of Napolean. The Carabinieri are easily identified by their colorful uniforms, especially by the red plumes on their three-cornered hats and by their swallow-tailed coats. Stefano's uncle will tell you that they perform their duties in pairs, very often on horseback, and that, like the Royal Canadian Mounties, they have a reputation for "always getting their man." Italians have their own nickname for them — "catch brothers."

Stefano will certainly remind you to visit the famous Fountain of Trevi in the capital city. A well-known legend has it that the visitor who throws a coin into its waters will return to Rome another day.

High in the gardens of the Villa Borghese, a couple have their picture taken with St. Peter's in the background

A water-color sketch of Frankfort Cathedral. In the foreground is the winding Main River

Germany

Long, long ago in northern Europe there were warlike tribes of people who lived in the forests. They also farmed and tended herds of sheep and cattle. Some tribes made war against the Roman armies and bitter campaigns followed with victories and losses on both sides. Later, when the Roman Empire began to weaken, these tribes — the Franks, Goths, Vandals, Lombards, Angles and Saxons — invaded many parts of Europe and founded new kingdoms. The years during which these wars were fought and the events which followed brought about many changes in Europe. One of these changes was the gradual emergence of Germany as a nation.

If you were to walk through some German cities now, you would

48

see that Germany has rebuilt almost all of the buildings ruined in World War II. Children on their way to school cross empty lots of rubble or go past brand-new buildings, many of which are extremely modern in design. The boys may be wearing lederhosen, which are sturdy leather shorts held by suspenders. Some of the younger boys wear gay Tyrolean jackets. They carry their books on their backs and their lunches in round tins. German mothers are noted for cleanliness in their homes and, even though they may still live in partly-ruined houses, their children are generally clean in appearance.

Oscar wears a knapsack to carry his schoolbooks

Two such boys living in Frankfort today are two brothers, thirteen-year-old Oscar and seven-year-old Hans Baier. Oscar and Hans can remember little else but the rebuilding that has been going on in their city all their lives. They will show you many interesting things in Frankfort which is on the Main River. It is one of the chief industrial cities of Europe. They will talk to you in English, too, for the boys have learned English at school and from American soldiers stationed there.

Wandering along the streets of the city you will see many stands which sell wurst, a close relative of the sausage known to Americans as frankfurters or hot dogs. Oscar will show you the house where Goethe, the famous poet, was born. His favorite place in the city is just below the rebuilt Frankfort cathedral, along the Main River. Here he sits and watches the barges and steamers that go down to the famous Rhine, the

river noted for its cliffs and beautiful castles. Along its green shores lived the Lorelei, a sorceress of legend, whose beauty and song lured many a ship and sailor to destruction.

Romantic Heidelberg, on the river Neckar, is famous for its castle and university. Mainz, standing where the Rhine joins the river of Mainz, is built on the site of an old Roman fort. The famous printer, Gutenberg, was born here. There is industrial Coblenz, an important commercial city, and Bonn, birthplace of the famous composer, Ludwig van Beethoven. Bonn is now the capital of the new German Federal Republic.

Germany's recent history, though not glorious, has been far from dull. Since her defeat in World War II she has been a country divided politically and geographically. Modeled after those countries that occupied her after the armistice, she now has a West Germany patterned after democratic Great Britain, France and the United States. East Germany bears the stamp of Russia and has a government consistent with those in the Communist countries. Berlin, Germany's capital, deep in the eastern sector, is also divided. In order to go from West Germany to West Berlin, a traveler must cross part of East Germany — and there has been trouble about this. Trouble has also grown out of the loss of thousands of Germans who fled East Germany. Seeking a better life for themselves, they escaped to the Western sector through Berlin. Then the East Germans built a solid brick wall around their sector of the city and permitted no one to leave without special permission.

Ancient Eschersheimer Tor still stands in modern rebuilt Frankfort

India

Imagine that your plane left New York just a day and a half ago. Soon you are winging over Calcutta, the largest port and industrial city in India. Down below is a busy sight of traffic-laden docks, tall smokestacks and a tremendous bridge that spans the river Hooghly. After landing at the Indian airport of Dum Dum, you are on your way to a hotel.

Once there, you will probably want to hire a guide. You can find one who will be at your side all day. At night he will sleep right outside your door. This is a long-established custom in India. Krishna, your new friend and guide, will speak English perfectly. During nearly 200 years of British rule in India, the English language became widespread and today it is the common language of all educated Indians.

Krishna will teach you to say hello in the Indian way, which is done by joining the hands at chest level, as in prayer. Few people in India greet each other by shaking hands, the way we do. He will tell you that although India has such big cities as Calcutta, Bombay,

52

Hyderabad and the capital, New Delhi, most of the people live in thousands of small villages throughout the country. Krishna will suggest that you visit such a village nearby to see how his countrymen live and how India is struggling to raise its standard of living.

Not far away the road widens and ahead you will see the low mud-colored huts that circle the village of Pradhar. Several oxen drink from a shallow pond close to a deep well. Nearby is a small white Hindu shrine. Some friends of Krishna live here and they have two children. Ram Das, the boy, is nine years old and Renu, his sister, is seven. They speak Bengali, their native tongue, but the children can also speak some Hindi, the official language of India, as well as a little English which they have learned in school.

Ram Das, Renu and their parents, Mr. and Mrs. Chatterjee, do not live in a thatched mud hut, but in a neat brick house with a bright red tiled roof and a tiny garden all around. Under a new construction program, houses in India are now made of stone or brick, for not only is wood scarce, but termites and heavy monsoon rains make wooden houses impracticable. Seated next to the fire in the kitchen, Renu helps her mother make "chappati," a pancake of wheat flour. Meat, vegetables or fish are eaten with rice or chappati and they are usually seasoned with a sharp curry sauce or

Ram Das stands before an ancient carved door

The Taj Mahal, one of the old wonders of the world

powder. Spoons or forks are very seldom used in the villages here.

Mr. Chatterjee, who owns fifteen acres of land, can tell you about India's development plans which are front-page talk everywhere in India. It is the nation's fight against hunger and disease. For some years the government has been sending teachers to outlying villages to give instruction in sanitation and health improvement. Technicians also come to teach the villagers how to build new schools, pave new roads and run more efficient farms. With the help of a government technician Mr. Chatterjee has been taught new ways of cultivating his land, and he is learning to keep bees in order to sell honey.

Krishna will tell you that India, once the land of spices and jute, of mystery, of fairy-tale palaces encrusted with gems, of elephants, tigers and cobra charmers and today, of modern industries, is in size a little more than a third of the United States. In population, however, India has more than twice as many people as the United States. With 440,000,000 people, or about one-seventh of the world's population, it is a crowded country. In India you can find as many as 200 different religions, about fifteen main languages and several hundred different dialects. India's history dates back almost 5,000 years.

India, long ago, had a rich and flourishing civilization and her magnificent cities were centers of learning, Mrs. Chatterjee will tell you. A period

54

of invasions by Huns, Arabs, Persians, Tartars and others followed. In more modern times, European powers, including the Portuguese, Dutch, French and English, competed with each other for trade in the East. When General Robert Clive, considered the founder of the British empire in India, defeated French forces and later, in 1757, won the important battle of Plassey, the British East India Company gained control of the country. But the Company's rule was often unjust and there were bitter rebellions by the Indians. In 1858, the British Government took over the rule from the East India Company. That rule lasted until 1947.

Today, Mr. Chatterjee will explain, India is an independent republic and a member of the British Commonwealth of Nations. The Indian constitution is modeled after that of the United States and the country is governed in a way that is similar to the American system of State and Federal government. Of the people who served India during the years of struggle for independence from

It takes four hours to dress a Jaipur elephant

Renu helps her mother sift flour

Great Britain, Mahatma Gandhi was by far the most outstanding. This Hindu was a spiritual as well as political leader. He preached peaceful methods in the Indian resistance to British rule. Pandit Jawaharlal Nehru, the nation's first prime minister, was another leading figure of the independence movement. Under his leadership India made important strides to raise its standard of living.

Ram Das has been learning something about the history of his country in school. He will tell you that India is made up of many states and provinces. Before August 15, 1947, India's day of independence, these areas were ruled by British governors, or Indian princes called maharajahs. One of the most picturesque of these states is Mysore, in southern India. There you can see how wild elephants are caught. A herd is surrounded by hundreds of men who make loud noises. The frightened animals are then easily driven into traps. Sometimes a tame and specially-trained elephant leads his wild brothers into captivity. A grand elephant procession in Mysore is also part of the Dusserah, a Hindu religious holiday celebrated each year all over India. The elephants, elaborately decorated, add color and excitement to the proceedings. It attracts many visitors.

You will learn from Krishna that Indian Hindus believe in reincarnation. This religious belief holds that the souls of dead people keep returning to earth in new bodies, either human or animal. This explains the great respect Hindus have for animals. You will learn also that you must remove your shoes before entering a holy place and that you must not bring in anything made of leather, for leather is made from the skin of an animal.

It is time to return to Calcutta and Mr. Chatterjee has consented to allow Ram Das and Renu to accompany you and Krishna back to the city. In a little while you are again in the crowded streets of Calcutta. Carts pulled by oxen or long-haired zebus move slowly side by side with old automobiles and sleek convertibles. Women wearing colorful saris, or cloth wrap-arounds, walk by gracefully, bracelets tinkling on their wrists and ankles, while next to them walk men wearing dhotis, or long loincloths, and bright turbans.

Bearded Sikhs, and Parsis whose ancestors came from Persia centuries ago, pick their way respectfully around a sacred cow lying in the street. Fortunetellers, merchants peddling tropical birds and small boys who would like you to buy their ivory trinkets are never very far away.

Down the street, animal trainers run their performing bears and monkeys through a series of tricks for the interested crowds. Their laughter blends with the Oriental tunes of the flute-playing snake charmers and with the tinkling of tambourines and bells. More common are wandering fakirs who beg for alms.

Much of what you see here is a part of the old way of life. But, as Krishna will remind you, India is slowly changing its ways and becoming a modern nation.

Courtyards are decorated on holidays with "rangoli," floor and wall designs made from colored rice paste mixture

Israel

Here is an old, old land which was reborn in 1948. It is also one of the world's real mysteries. People for centuries have wondered why, with the whole world from which to choose, fate chose this particular stony soil to give birth to three great religions — Judaism, Christianity and Mohammedanism.

Perhaps you will go to Israel by ship, which will dock in the fine harbor at Haifa. This seaport city, situated on the shore of the Bay

58

of Acre at the foot of Mount Carmel, is over 2,000 years old. The friendly Israeli people will greet you in Hebrew, the ancient language of the Bible, which is being spoken again in this tiny country. You will soon learn that "shalom," which means "peace," is an all-purpose greeting. One of your welcomers might very well be fourteen-year-old David Miron who is anxious to practice the English he has learned in school.

David was born in Europe and he survived the tragedies of World War II. Brought with other homeless children to his new home in Israel, he is now living in one of the many villages for children scattered throughout this tiny land. He will surely invite you to visit him there and meet his "family." And what a family—more than one hundred children — all of them orphans! Rescued from the war, many of them arrived ill and were made well. They studied, worked and played — they learned about planting, harvesting and the care of animals, and they grew strong and sturdy. If you ask David what his job is, he will tell you proudly that he is the sheepherder of the village, just as the Biblical King David was centuries ago.

David has been visiting friends and he is on his way back to his

Off through the hot sun to the children's swimming pool

village near Jerusalem. You will be going in that direction and David has accepted your invitation to travel together. In a little while your porter, a tall Yemenite Jew, loads your baggage into a taxi for the trip south to Tel Aviv, another seaside city of Israel.

Tel Aviv is the largest city in the country and it is also the most modern in that part of the world. You will see many new apartment houses there with balconies that look out over the Mediterranean Sea. Several roads lead from Tel Aviv to other places, some of which even existed in Biblical times. There are roads that lead to the rolling Judean Hills, to the southern desert — called the Negev — and to the fertile plain of Sharon.

Later, on the bus to Jerusalem, David will tell you that long ago Israel, or the "Land of Canaan," as the ancient Hebrews called it, was the home of the Jewish people and the birthplace of the stories and laws of the Old Testament. Also, it was here in Bethlehem, in a small manger, that a child was born — a child Who grew up to teach His followers the ways of Christianity.

After repeated invasions by many peoples and the destruction of their homes and the Temple of Jerusalem by the Romans, the Jews were forced to flee to other countries. A period of Arab control was followed by the capture of Jerusalem by the Crusaders, but Moslem rule was soon restored and Mohammedanism grew. Later, control of

A view of Old Jerusalem —
as seen from New Jerusalem

Palestine, as it became known, was transferred to Turkey.

After World War I, the League of Nations gave a mandate to Great Britain to govern Palestine. The League was in favor of making it a home for Jews. Thus encouraged, the Jews bought land from Arabs living there and slowly the desert dunes, barren swamps and sandy hills began to change. Up sprang towns and villages, orchards and groves and even factories. Men, women and bright-faced children worked hard to fulfill their ancient dream of restoring Israel. They dreamed also of making a haven here for those who were fleeing from religious persecution and intolerance elsewhere.

Soon the bus passes Zorah, where Samson, the Israelite judge who had great physical strength, was born. Later, David will point out the valley of Elah where young David killed the Philistine giant, Goliath. You can make out the ruins of a truck half-hidden in clumps of wild blooming poppies. It is a reminder of the Arab-Israeli war of 1948 when Arabs from six neighboring countries invaded Israel after that tiny nation proclaimed her independence.

The United States was the first country to recognize the new nation. However, the surrounding Arab countries considered all of Palestine Arab territory and, disregarding a United Nations vote to separate Palestine into Arab and Jewish states, they tried to

On Mt. Zion, an elderly scribe copies ancient scrolls

Yemenite girls still wear silver filigreed hoods on holidays

David is taught building and masonry

61

Azmi el Gamel, David's Arab friend, wears a tarboosh

push the new settlers into the sea. But a modern miracle occurred and the Israelis, outnumbered six to one, held off the invaders and kept their freedom. Then, in 1949, the state of Israel was admitted to the United Nations.

Soon the bus arrives in Jerusalem, the capital of Israel and a city which is holy to Christians, Jews and Moslems. As you and David wander through the New City of Jerusalem, past limestone buildings, handsome hotels, low houses and winding streets, you will see, sprinkled among the buildings, small fields of gnarled olive trees. Because the Old City of Jerusalem is in Jordan, and the Arabs forbid crossing over into it from the New City of Jerusalem on the Israeli side, David would probably take you up to the top of the Y.M.C.A.

From its high tower, you can see over the ancient walls and into the Old City. David will point out the Church of the Holy Sepulcher. Farther back is the site of the Temple of Solomon. Nearby you can

An old mosque in Israel

see the dark blue dome of the Mosque of Omar, hiding the rock where Abraham prepared to sacrifice his son, Isaac, to God. That green hill, David will tell you, pointing to the southeast, is the Mount of Olives, and ancient Bethlehem lies near the horizon.

To the right of the Old City, on Israeli soil, is the sacred hill of Zion, where the tomb of King David lies. Far to the south, where Israel is making the dry lands of the Negev desert bloom, are the ancient mines of King Solomon. Men are digging there even today. Not too far away is the Dead Sea, whose waters are so salty that you can float without even trying. Along the Dead Sea is Sodom, the wicked city of Biblical history. From the newly revived port of Elath, Israel's gateway to the Indian Ocean, King Solomon sent his ships to the Queen of Sheba and to distant lands to trade copper and other products. Turning now to the north, David will point out the location of quiet Acre whose

This is believed to be the site of Joseph's carpentry shop

fortresses, some built by Alexander the Great, defied even the Crusaders and, centuries later, Napoleon.

As David points out historic spots, an Arab family in the street below walks slowly behind their tiny donkey, which the father rides. "Don't be surprised," David will tell you. "Israel has quite a number of Arab families living here. In fact, Nazareth, the village where Christ lived as a child, is occupied entirely by Christian and Moslem Arabs." Nazareth is Israel's largest completely Arab city.

Descending from the high tower, David will tell you of his friend, Azmi el Gamel. Azmi is an Arab boy who lives in Nazareth, and he is also fourteen years old. As you walk with David down the sunny street you will probably stop for a drink of orange juice. Israeli Jaffa oranges, named after the city where Jonah took a ship before he was swallowed by a whale, are delicious. Oranges and other citrus fruits grown in the ancient city of Jaffa are exported all over the world.

As you say "shalom" to bid "good-by" to David, you will have Azmi's address in your pocket and directions for traveling north to Arab Nazareth. Nazareth is in a lovely section of the country known as the Lower Galilee. Once there you will see a small village that clings to the slope of a hill. Modern buildings, paved streets and electric street lights stand next to ancient Biblical sites. Along its main street, lined with shops and cafes, you will see Arab men smoking Oriental pipes called narghiles and drinking tiny cups of thick dark coffee.

Azmi's house is a humble single-room dwelling with a raised platform where the family eats by day and sleeps by night, sharing the room with chickens, sheep and goats. Perhaps, as many Biblical scholars believe, it is similar to the one where the Christ child was born. Azmi and his family will welcome you to their country, too, for Moslems, as well as Christians and Jews, are citizens of Israel.

Arab smoking a pipe called a narghile

As you wait with Azmi to cross the road and begin your sight-seeing, a slow-moving line of camels goes by, followed by a flock of sheep. You will notice the flowing garments worn by the Arabs. If you admire Azmi's white linen headdress, he will tell you that it is called a kafia.

Azmi will also tell you that when Christ lived here, Nazareth was a very busy community, and along these very streets was the synagogue where Christ and other Jewish children studied.

At sundown you and Azmi will hear the wailing song of the muezzin as he calls the Moslems of Nazareth to prayer from a high minaret. "Salam aleikum," says Azmi in Arabic, "and when you return to Jerusalem, say 'shalom' to David for me."

Woman fetching water at M a r y ' s W e l l

Peat for fuel is for sale everywhere in Ireland

Ireland

This is the Emerald Isle of lovely ancient names, of fairies and leprechauns and of wondrously tall tales. Indeed, if you are lucky enough to kiss the Blarney Stone, legend has it that you, too, will be able to spin stories as tall and convincing as the native Irish. Some say this legend applies only to men, for the Blarney Stone is located near the top of the wall of ancient Blarney Castle, and it is very difficult to reach.

Bustling Shannon Airport, just outside the city of Limerick, is a stopping place for transatlantic planes, and Limerick is a good point from which you may begin a tour of Ireland. The city, lying on both sides of the Shannon River, is the chief port on the west coast of Eire. Eire is an ancient Gaelic word for Ireland. It usually refers to the Republic of Ireland, but not to Northern Ireland which is a part of the United Kingdom of Great Britain.

You will find that almost everyone speaks English. English and Gaelic are the two official languages of the country. It won't be long before someone asks shyly if you are from the same city in the United States where he has relatives. You might be, since there are four times as many people of Irish descent in the United States as there are in Ireland. In fact, New York City has the largest Irish population of any city in the entire world.

During the 1840's the crops failed in Ireland and there was a great famine. Many Irish came to America seeking new means of livelihood. The letters they sent home to their families and friends helped to make stronger the bonds of friendship between the United States and Ireland.

In Limerick someone will surely urge you to visit the picturesque city of Galway, which is farther north in County Galway. The ride there will be along lovely blue-green fields of grass and through a poetry of names: Newmarket-on-Fergus, Clarecastle, Ennis, Crusheen, Derrybrien, Kinvara, Oranmore and many others.

Two Irish boys who stop to watch as you photograph Maureen, a lovely Galway lass wearing a woven shawl, are Michael Gannon and Thomas O'Dea. Both are eleven-year-olds who live in the Claddagh. Claddagh is a Gaelic word meaning "stoney

Michael Gannon and Thomas O'Dea

beach." It is a part of the city of Galway and is inhabited mostly by fishermen. Michael and Thomas will tell you that their fathers are fishermen, as were their fathers before them, and that the salmon caught here is the best in all of Ireland.

The boys will tell you that because of its fine harbor, Galway has become one of the most important seaports in the country. The city began as a fort, and there are many old buildings to be found here.

Lynch's Castle, which has a central courtyard, is Spanish in style. St. Nicholas Church, a cross-shaped building, and the Franciscan monastery, are two of the oldest buildings in Galway. One of the best schools, they will tell you, is University College, a college of the National University of Ireland. Michael and Thomas would like to go there some day.

They will show you the Spanish Arch which is a reminder of the days of Spanish settlement in Ireland. But best of all, you will like the quaint thatched cottages that may still be seen along the Irish countryside.

Mike and Tom like to watch the playing of hurling, a game similar to field hockey. Their sport of football, another favorite, is like the American game. Both boys are in their seventh year at St. Nicholas' School. They study mathematics, geography, Irish history, Gaelic, English and music. They also receive religious instruction.

They know much about Irish history and will tell you about the Celts who settled in Ireland over 2,000 years ago. It was St. Patrick who brought Christianity to Ireland in the fifth century. For many years warfare and bitterness raged between Ireland and England. Finally, the English won absolute

A common sight — black shawls in southern Ireland

control when, in 1800, the Act of Union bound together the two countries as the "United Kingdom of Great Britain and Ireland." However, many Irish fought for an end to the British laws governing them. When Britain offered Ireland dominion status, only the northern counties accepted. Northern Ireland became a part of Great Britain. The southern counties, which had opposed British rule for many years, refused. In 1937, Ireland became an independent state, and in 1949 it gained complete freedom from Great Britain.

Dublin is the capital and largest city in Ireland. Its location and fine harbor make it the country's leading port for trade with Great Britain and other countries. Dublin means "black pool," the name once given to that part of the Liffey River on which the city lies.

Tom and Mike must have kissed the Blarney Stone because their soft voices are easy to listen to as they tell you about harvesting flax, riding to hounds at Tipperary, and about the curious stone formation in Antrim, Northern Ireland, known as the Giant's Causeway. But when they describe the horse fairs at Galway and at Connemara, you will learn that selling a horse in Ireland is sealed with a great shout and a firm handclasp. There is no place for soft words then!

Ink sketch of the Spanish Arch in Galway

Morro Castle in the harbor of Havana

Cuba

Five centuries ago, on the 28th of October, 1492, Christopher Columbus sighted the swaying palm trees of Cuba. It is said that he sighed and declared, "This is the loveliest land that human eyes have ever seen."

Columbus was amazed by the tropical beauty he found and, if you were to visit Cuba today, you would be amazed, too. Imagine finding a fruit vendor in busy Havana selling heavy coconuts, enormous bunches of bananas, fragrant oranges, pineapples, papayas, ripe watermelons, avocados, mangoes, mamoneillos, cantaloupes, large cucumbers and giant eggplants — all on a corner stand. You may even try to memorize the names of the new fruits as you drink a glass of cool coconut milk.

If you stand near Public School No. 154, just down the street, when school lets out, you are likely to meet eight-year-old Juan Antonio Caraballo-Pita. In his bulging brief case Juan has books on arithmetic, history, Spanish, drawing and manual arts. He studies music also, but he is really best in Cuban history.

Cuba is the largest island in the West Indies and it is one of a group known as the Greater Antilles. It is less than an hour by plane from the southern tip of Florida and it is not too far east of Mexico. Jamaica, Haiti, the Dominican Republic and Puerto Rico, a free commonwealth nation associated with the United States, make up the rest of this group.

Farther along these waters, which once saw the passing red sails of slave ships and the black flags of buccaneers, are smaller islands known as the

Cathedral Square in Havana, once the burial site of Christopher Columbus

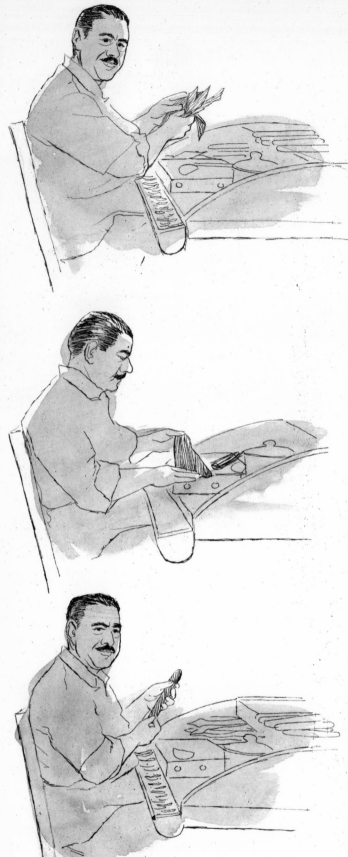

Señor Caraballo-Pita makes a cigar

Lesser Antilles. There, amongst others, are the islands of Martinique and Guadeloupe, where the weird rites of voodoo are still practiced. There, too, is Trinidad, where tall, graceful dancers do calypsos in the streets to the sounds of music from old tin cans and gasoline drums.

You can picnic in Tobago, Juan tells you, on the very island where Robinson Crusoe sat and watched for a white sail on the bright blue sea. Off the northern tip of Tobago is Juan's favorite place, tiny Ingram Island, or Bird of Paradise Island, as it is also called. The rare and beautiful birds of paradise can be seen there by the thousands. At a farther point, almost touching South America, is Curacao.

Walking home with Juan along the Malecon Drive, the seacoast highway of Havana, you might meet his father, Señor Caraballo-Pita, who is going home for lunch. He and Juan will point out Morro Castle, a famous fort guarding the harbor of Havana. It was here, in 1898, that the American battleship, the *U. S. S. Maine* was blown up. The Spanish-American War followed and Cuba, then a colony of Spain, was freed after the defeat of Spain by the United States. She became an independent nation and a republic in 1902.

Since that time, Cuba has had democratic governments as well as dictatorships. In 1959, one dictatorship was overthrown and replaced by a government still using military force for its survival. Great restrictions were imposed on Cubans. Many Cubans fled to the United States. They hope one day to return to a democratic country. In 1961 the United States broke off diplomatic relations with Cuba to protest the confiscation of American properties and the violation of the rights of those Americans living there.

If digging for treasure interests you, Juan could tell you about the island off Cuba called the Isle of Pines. This, it is said, is the Treasure Island made famous by Robert Louis Stevenson and, some day soon, Juan expects to do some treasure-digging of his own.

Not only does Cuba produce enough sugar to supply the whole world, but it also grows some of the world's finest tobacco. Juan's father is a master cigar-maker who started making hand-made cigars at the age of fourteen. Cigar-makers keep up with the latest news and a great deal of other information by listening to a reader whose special job is to read to them while they are at work. Men all over the world have smoked his cigars, Señor Caraballo-Pita will tell you proudly, including the noted English statesman, Sir Winston Churchill.

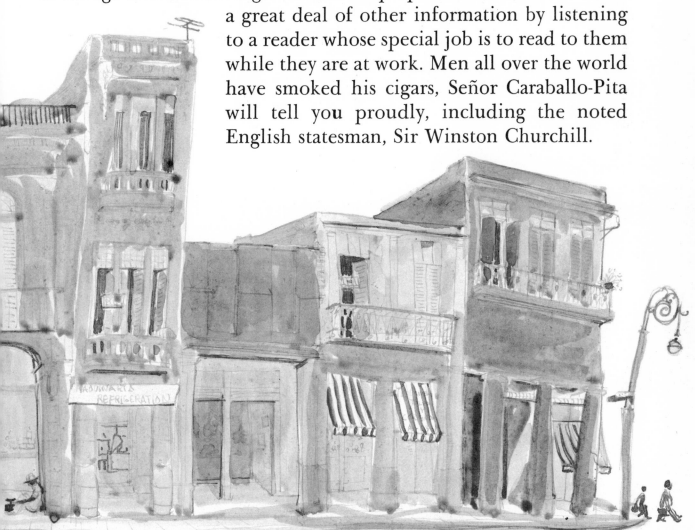

Walking home from school. Note the TV antenna

First day of school in Moscow

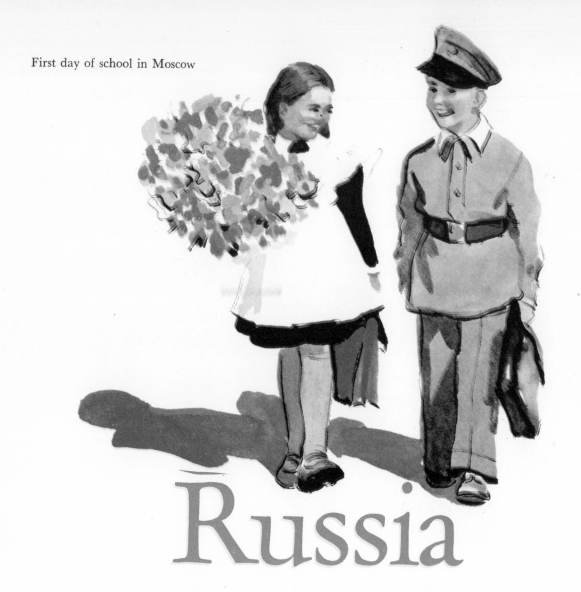

Russia

The Union of Soviet Socialist Republics, which almost everyone calls Russia, or the Soviet Union, or by the initials USSR, is the largest country in the world. Almost three times the size of the United States, the USSR covers about one-sixth of the earth's surface. Within her borders live over 200 million people. Always an important nation, she has also recently loomed as a strong one. Travelers speak differently of the impression it makes on them — "exciting," "depressing," "bright," "dull," "open," "stifling," — but most agree that the Russian people themselves are very friendly.

Moscow, the capital of the USSR, is a good place for you to see some of the citizens that make up this giant country, and Red Square, in the very center of the city, is an appropriate spot from which to begin. As you arrive, the guards are changing in front of the huge red granite tomb of Nikolai Lenin, one of the strong leaders of the revolution of 1917. Day after day, in all kinds of weather, the faithful and curious from everywhere will line up to view the preserved body lying in state.

Just behind you, a boy dressed in a blue sailor suit waits in line with his drably-dressed mother and father. His mother is curious about your clothes and admires their quality and style. The line inches forward slowly and soon you are making friends with them. Mr. and Mrs. Danilov and their nine-year-old son Sergei are sight-seeing in Moscow, and Sergei has looked forward to this trip for months. Sergei's father knows the capital well, and his English, which he learned at school, is good. During World War II, he learned many American expressions while serving as a guide for visiting American soldiers and officials.

"Women work at everything here," says Sergei in answer to your question about the busy-looking grandmother sweeping

The colorful towers of St. Basil's Cathedral in Red Square

Soviet Cossacks in Turkistan
hunt even now with falcons

the street with a quaint twig broom. "And they do a good job, too," he adds.

The Danilovs point out a medieval cathedral with painted, onion-shaped turrets near Red Square. They will tell you that the Cathedral of St. Basil was built four centuries ago during the reign of Ivan the Terrible. It is so beautiful that it is now being restored because of its artistic qualities. However, the government does not encourage religious worship. In fact, the Soviet government has turned some churches into anti-religious museums.

Soon Sergei is telling you shyly about himself. At school he studies many of the subjects that American schools teach, including foreign languages like English. You may be surprised to hear that Sergei studies more scientific courses than does an American boy his own age. Sergei's father would like him to be a scientist. If he is able to pass his examinations, he may become a member of this most sought-after group of Soviet workers. After his education is complete, he may be sent to work for two years in any place in the vast country to repay the state for his free schooling.

Sergei has many uniforms. When he goes to school he wears a soldier suit with long pants and visor cap. Now that he has joined a group known as the "Little Octobrists" he may wear another uniform with a flowing red tie. Later he may become a "Young Pioneer." Millions of boys and girls belong to these clubs and meet to sing, hike, parade and go camping. This spring Sergei will probably march down Red Square with his club members to be reviewed by the men who rule Russia. The rulers of the country make their headquarters in the Kremlin, whose massive red brick walls face Red Square.

Sergei will tell you that there are about 170 nationalities in the

USSR today and about 200 different languages and dialects. Teaching children to understand Russian in the USSR is a big job. Later in the day Sergei's father will take you through the elegant subway, of which the Muscovites are quite proud. He will point out the new buildings that are slowly replacing the old slums of Moscow.

Sergei will tell you about the sands of the Turkmen Republic that are hot enough on which to fry eggs, and of the coldest spot on earth in northeast Siberia where the temperature once dipped to ninety degrees below zero. The USSR is a country where you can see an atomic reactor in operation, but where there are no detailed city maps or directories or telephone books for public use.

If it is early enough, the Danilovs may invite you to visit their home. Sergei's grandparents live with them in a small suburb of Moscow. Over a delicious bowl of borsht, or beet soup, mixed with sour cream, Grandfather Danilov will tell you of Russia's great writers and musicians. The writings of Tolstoy, Chekhov, Pushkin and Gogol, and the music of Rimski-Korsakov, Tchaikovsky, Borodin and Shostakovich bring delight to people everywhere.

Soon hot tea is being served from a small electric samovar on the table, together with delicious little baked pies filled with apples, called "piroshki." Later, Sergei may challenge his father to a game of chess, the most popular game in the Soviet Union today. It is a quiet game and Sergei is still trying to find ways to checkmate his father in three moves. But much as he enjoys playing chess, there is something which he enjoys even more — reading about rockets and the latest scientific achievements in outer space.

The TU-104, a Soviet passenger jet

Nikos and Maria
dressed as evzones

Greece

Jutting into the Mediterranean between the Ionian and the Aegean Seas are the 437 islands which make up modern Greece. This is "sailors' country" where almost everyone knows the sea. No spot of land in any direction is more than about seventy-five miles from a coast. This is the part of the world that gave us heroes, myths and legends galore. Its ancient art, literature and knowledge have stirred human minds and hearts for centuries.

The heavens where Prometheus stole fire to give to man; the hills where Hercules battled the lion; the seas in which Ulysses struggled through the terrible tempests; Sparta, the home of beautiful Helen who fled with Paris to Troy; and Mount Parnassus, where the steep trail can still be seen that leads up to the sacred places of Apollo and the Muses — all are here.

In the modern city of Athens are the ruins of the ancient capital of Greece which have inspired artists and architects for centuries. The Parthenon, the famous temple sacred to the goddess Athena, is the most popular place at which to start your sight-seeing tour. As you climb the Acropolis, a hill about 260 feet high, where the white columns of the ruins look down on the new city below, you might see two strangely-dressed Greek children who, with their father, are also taking a sight-seeing trip.

Remains of the 2,500-year-old Propylaea, entrance to the Acropolis

Nicholas, nicknamed Nikos, and Maria Bakirtis are both dressed in the white uniform of the evzones, the crack Greek riflemen recruited from the mountain regions. This costume is usual with Greek children on holidays, and today is a holiday. Mr. Bakirtis, who speaks English, explains that he and the children have come from the nearby seaside town of Glyfada to spend the day in Athens. He will tell you that this Doric temple, the 2,500-year-old Parthenon, which you see on top of the Acropolis, has been restored by Greek architects. A reproduction of the Parthenon stands today in Nashville, Tennessee.

Looking down from the Acropolis, Mr. Bakirtis will point out the ruins of a Greek amphitheater. Here under the stars, for the amphitheater never had a roof, the ancient Greeks performed their stirring plays and held great oratorical and dramatic contests. Slowly descending the Acropolis, Mr. Bakirtis will also point to the streets below where Pericles, Socrates, Plato and Aristotle used to walk. "Look out to sea and there's the old seaport of Piraeus that still plays host to ships from all over the world," he will say.

Once below, Nikos and Maria beg their father for a sweet to share with you. From a street vendor he buys everyone a generous slice of baklava, a honey-and-nut pastry. As you lick the sweet honey from your fingers, Nikos, who is twelve, will inform you

A windmill typical of the island of Mykonos, a popular resort area

shyly that at school he is studying algebra, history, chemistry, ancient Greek, geography and the Bible. If you were to accept their invitation to visit Glyfada, you would be surprised to see that their school, which greatly resembles our own grade schools, has lovely pink- and blue-striped pillars. Saturday is also a school day here.

Maria, who is ten, knows her country well and she can tell you that Greek olives, wine, figs and tobacco are exported all over the world. These exports are important to the Greeks who are recovering from the terrible hardships they suffered during World War II when German troops occupied their country. After Greece was liber-

Have your picture taken against the ruins of the Arch of Hadrian

ated, a civil war raged in the country, which resulted in a victory for the democratic side. Today Greece is a constitutional monarchy.

Nikos will tell you that some of the other large cities in Greece are Salonica, Corfu, Piraeus and Patras. One of his favorite places is ancient Peloponnesos, which is a peninsula forming the southern part of the Greek mainland. On that island is Olympia, the site of the first Olympian games. The ruins of the stadium, where games and races were held centuries ago, can still be seen there. Athletes and spectators from all Greece went to Olympia every four years to celebrate the national and religious festival that honored the mighty god Zeus. The Olympic games are now an international event. Athletes from many parts of the world meet every fourth year in a different country and compete with each other in various sports.

Farther west are the snow-capped peaks of Mount Olympus where the Greek gods of legend are reported to have dwelled. Sometimes, Nikos and Maria like to pretend that the gods are still there.

Per Lars wears a Lapp hat and jacket

Norway

So far north that it is called "The Land of The Midnight Sun," is a Scandinavian country measuring over 1,100 miles in length. The sea pokes deep fingers into the coast, forming fjords, or narrow inlets in the mountains from whose snow-topped peaks flow steady streams of water. This free source of water power has given Norway more electricity for each of her people than any nation in the world.

A giant backbone range of mountains called Kjölen, meaning the "keel," runs north and south along Norway's eastern border. The gentle, broad valleys and farmlands of the east country that border Sweden are quite different from the fjord- and island-studded coast of the west country. In the west, Norway has many days of wind and rain each year, but fortunately, warm ocean currents keep the ports free from ice the year round.

Eight-year-old Per Lars can tell you what it is like to live in a mountainous country where children learn to ski almost as soon as they can walk. It is a land where hay is hung out lovingly to dry in the sun and then sent scooting down the mountainside by wire slides to the barns below. Far in the north country you can see the Lapp people tend their reindeer herds, just as their ancestors did before them generations ago.

Last year Per, who lives in Oslo, capital of Norway, was delighted to have his cousins from America come to visit him. He even posed for a color snapshot while wearing a Lapp hat and coat so that his cousins might have a souvenir photograph of their visit to Norway. On their first Sunday, after a breakfast which included milk and goat cheese, Per was ready to show them the sights of the city.

On the way to one of the many fine museums in Oslo, Per told them all about his hero Thor Heyerdahl who, with five companions, crossed the Pacific Ocean on a raft named *Kon-Tiki*. They proved that the people of ancient Peru could have sailed to the South Sea islands on similar rafts. The *Kon-Tiki*, which drifted over 4,000 miles, is now exhibited in the Kon-Tiki Museum

The waterfall of the Seven Sisters tumbles 1,500 feet. Hay dries beside a typical Norwegian sod-roofed barn

in Bygdoy, a suburb of Oslo. Another hero of his is the Norwegian statesman, Trygve Lie, who was the first Secretary-General of the United Nations.

Some of the sleek wooden ships of the Vikings are preserved at the Viking Ship Museum. Long ago, warlike Norsemen from Norway raided the coastal cities of Europe for booty, and many settled in what is now Ireland and the Normandy region of France. In the year 1000, Leif Ericsson sailed across the then unknown seas and discovered a part of North America which the Norse voyagers called Vinland. Norway became a united kingdom in 872, and since the thirteenth century has been an important nation. Its history, for many centuries, has been tied to that of her Scandinavian cousins and neighbors, Sweden and Denmark.

As they wandered down the tree-lined main street of Oslo, Per showed his cousins the University of Oslo, the National Theater, and the Storthing, where Norway's Parliament meets. They could see the royal palace which is situated high on a hill. King Haakon VII was the sovereign of the democratic Norwegian government for over fifty years until his death in 1957. During this time Norway developed a special program to help the sick and to care for needy and elderly

Norway produces more whale oil than any other country in the world. Here is the first step in processing the blubber

people. This program has served as a model for many other countries.

Per took his cousins to lunch at lovely Frogner Park in the capital city. There they ate sandwiches of delicious fat Norwegian herrings. After lunch they strolled in the park and admired the beautiful statues of the famous sculptor, Vigeland. Per told of the time he took a cable railway to the top of one of the seven high mountains that overlook the city of Bergen. He will never forget the beautiful view there of the harbor, the fjords and the forest of fishing-boat masts.

Children in Norway are taught the usual subjects during their seven years of elementary school. In addition, there is carpentry for the boys, and sewing, knitting and cooking for the girls. In their last two years they begin to study English.

Per likes to play "stikkball," derived from stickball, which is similar to American baseball. Norwegians love athletics and out-of-doors activity. Skiing and ice skating are their two most popular winter sports. The most exciting month of the year for Per Lars is March when an annual week-long series of ski events is held in the Holmenkollen Hills on the outskirts of Oslo. This is called Holmenkollen Week, and on the last day, there is a ski-jump contest. You can be sure that Per will be there, watching with great interest.

Lucienne Van Houte holds the bobbin lace she made by hand

Belgium

Over 2,000 years ago, the Roman general Julius Caesar conquered a tribe of people who lived in what is now the Kingdom of Belgium. The tribe was known as the Belgae and it is from them that one of the smallest countries in Europe got its name. The nation has a long history and some of her leading cities date back hundreds of years. In spite of modern times, which brings with it new buildings and new ways of manufacturing products, the people of Belgium have managed to preserve much of their old way of life.

Such a contrast between the old and the new may be seen in the

old city of Bruges. Walking through one of the picturesque streets you will come to a tiny schoolhouse where young girls are taught the old Flemish specialty of making bobbin lace from flax, by hand. A design is made on a parchment pattern, which is then pinned on a pillow. The girls, working rapidly, weave the threads among the pins. The result is a ribbon of snow-white bobbin lace, more beautiful than any machine can make.

In years past mothers taught their daughters the old patterns, but many of the rare designs were nearly forgotten. To revive and preserve the art, the city of Bruges established a school for girls who study lace-making after their regular school hours. If you were to stop by any afternoon after four, you would see eight-year-old Lucienne Van Houte in her clean, white smock, working busily. Lucienne is an expert lace-maker with three years of training. She has lived in Bruges all her life.

Walking home through the century-old streets, past ancient treasure houses, is a daily treat for Lucienne, and she can tell you a great deal about her city. Bruges is only a few miles from the North Sea and about fifty-five miles northwest of Brussels. For many years it has been a favorite place for tourists because of its beautiful paintings and statues, its quaint medieval buildings, scenic bridges and picturesque canals. It was once Belgium's chief port and trade center, but today, Antwerp is the country's chief seaport.

If Lucienne invites you to her home to meet her grandmother, you will make your way along some of those colorful bridges which pass over the many lovely canals in Bruges. On the way, you may pass a Belgian

Beginners learn lace-making on these outsized spindles

A quiet canal in Bruges

wagon, or dray, drawn by robust Brabantine horses. These are still among the world's finest animals. As you stroll in the dusk, forty-seven bells housed in the belfry tower of the old Market Hall will ring out a Flemish folk tune. Every fifteen minutes the tower clock sets the carillon in motion, as it has done since the eighteenth century.

Lucienne has traveled to many other cities in Belgium and she can tell you about them. Antwerp is an old artistic city and one of Europe's great seaports. The home and studio of Peter Paul Rubens, the famous painter, are preserved there as a museum. In fact, there are many museums in Belgium, and in Brussels, the capital city, a street car has been nicknamed "the museum local." Twelve miles south of Brussels is the village of Waterloo, where Napoleon slept on the eve of his fateful battle, and where Victor Hugo wrote the famous novel "Les Misérables."

As you cross one of the canals and turn left, you will see some elderly ladies sitting at their doorsteps in the quiet square, weaving lace patterns. One grandmother wearing a lace cap bends over her little cushioned stand, clicking her wooden bobbin. With flying fingers she quickly adds another bit to her roll of lace.

She is Lucienne's grandmother and she will speak to you in Flemish, which is a language much like Dutch. Lucienne will tell you that both French and Flemish are the official languages of the country. The people in the northern half of the country who speak Flemish are called Flemings. In the southern half of Belgium, the people speak a French dialect known as Walloon, and they are called Walloons. Later, as you say good-by, you might be lucky and receive a delicate, handmade lace doily from Lucienne's grandmother. It will be a perfect remembrance of your visit.

Lucienne's grandmother weaves a lace pattern

Portugal

Until recently this mountainous country on the western part of the Iberian Peninsula, next door to Spain, was not often visited by tourists. Today, air travel has made Lisbon, the capital of Portugal, an important airport center. Now travelers can stop for a visit and relax in the pleasant climate of this Portuguese-speaking land.

Lisbon, rebuilt after a devastating earthquake in 1755, is spread over seven hills. From a high vantage point, you can look down on long lines of picturesque houses painted in soft pastel colors. Some streets are paved with black stones that spell out important names in Portuguese history. The blue sea is a beautiful sight and Lisbon's harbor is one of the best in the world.

Before long you might meet someone like dark-eyed, twelve-year-old José do Rosario Ferreira Horta, from the nearby fishing village of Cascais. He has come to Lisbon to see one of Portugal's most exciting celebrations, which takes place every year. It is a time when the fishing boats set off for distant waters and José will invite you to stroll with him down to the Tagus River where the festival takes place.

On the way, you and José will walk through ancient narrow streets, and past old castle walls built by the Moors who once lived in Portugal. You will find that Lisbon also has modern boulevards, houses and schools. Because the city lies on hills or terraces, you can use the "ascensores," or elevators to take you up to the top. It costs less than a penny and many people prefer to use them instead of walking up the very steep steps.

Soon you will see the famous Tower of Belem in the middle of the Tagus River. It was built in the year 1500 as a monument to the sailors of Portugal. José will tell you that Portugal's seafaring men filled their country's history with adventure and glory. Vasco da Gama, the

José do Rosario Ferreira Horta of Cascais. Behind him is a fisherman's wife on her way to market

famous navigator, was the first man to sail around Africa and reach India by sea. The Tower of Belem marks the spot where this famous seaman and his crew set sail on their voyage in 1497. Portugal was a world power several centuries ago.

At the river you will see the Portuguese in their bright plaid shirts and gay print dresses. They have come to see the great fishing fleet set sail for Greenland and Nova Scotian waters. Special masses are sung, elaborate processionals are held and then there is the final blessing as the flag-draped boats slowly sail away. José will tell you that when he is sixteen years old, he would like to attend the free school for boys who want to become fishermen. Portuguese fish are exported to many countries and the ancient profession of the fisherman continues to be an honorable one.

José will tell you that in his village, on a Sunday, you can see dozens of fishermen in rubber boots and colorful stocking caps, mending nets. Here and there, hanging in bunches like overgrown grapes, are the painted pig-bladders that the men use as floats for their fishing nets. On Sundays, too, young women like to dress in gay ancestral costumes and promenade along the wide quay.

Perhaps you and José will hear one of the girls singing a "fado," which may tell a sad story about the sea, or perhaps you will hear a "vira" or a "chula," which are the more lively Portuguese dancing songs.

José likes to play with his friends in the warm sun along the beach of Cascais. Mountains cover two-thirds of his sun-baked country. Wheat is the principal crop, and only one-third of the land is fertile enough to be cultivated. Portugal is one of the world's important wine-makers, and a leading producer of cork. Her fishing industry, especially sardines, has been of special importance to the Portuguese economy. Green valleys, vineyards, orange and almond groves, grazing goats on green mountainsides, and a coast line of jagged rocks and clean sandy beaches make up some of Portugal's colorful setting.

José says that when he becomes a master fisherman he hopes to sail on one of the boats that visit the fishing beds off Nova Scotia. Then, as others have done before him, he wants to sail south to visit the United States. José has relatives, now American citizens, who live along the coast of New England. They fish out of such places as Gloucester and Cape Cod, and the bright plaid shirts they love to wear are constant reminders of Portugal, their ancestral homeland.

Sunday dress for girls in Cascais

A Portuguese fisherman

Spain

Some day, perhaps, you may be in Spain during Holy Week when solemn and beautiful religious ceremonies are held. Then, right after the celebration of Easter, Spain becomes the scene of yet another celebration. This is the "feria," the festival day, and street parties are held in many cities. In Seville, there is one party that lasts for an entire week, both days and nights.

In some cities you will see strange carnival figures made of wood, wax and papier-mâché. They are sometimes thirty feet high, and have very gay costumes that are covered with ornaments. These puppets are paraded in the streets during the day and, at night, with

94   The Alcázar in Seville

Seville's houses are topped by the classic mirador, turrets painted in bright colors

fireworks crackling and sparkling, they are burned in huge bonfires. Dancing in the light of their flames are young men wearing boleros and stiff-brimmed hats. Young girls, long flounces on their skirts, combs in their hair and shawls covering their shoulders, dance, too.

In Selville, dancing with the other boys and girls of her street, is María Teresa Carretero Munoz, who is six years old. Her face is very serious, her tiny castanets click, her heels stamp and her skirt flies about gaily. She is dancing the flamenco, an Andalusian Gypsy dance. Some people say that this dance came from the Moors who occupied the country long ago.

Andalusia is a part of southern Spain and here, in the land of orange trees, olives and grapes, palm trees and flowered patios, the old Spanish dances are still being taught. If, on your way to the Plaza de Toros, where the bullfights take place, you and María stop to listen at an open door, you will surely hear clicking castanets and the wild, sad music of the flamenco.

The Spaniards are a very proud and proper people. It will be necessary, therefore, for you to be introduced formally to Señor Carretero before he will allow María and you to become friends. But after the introduction, you will find them very kind and hospitable. María is the only child of Señor and Señora Carretero Munoz and they are determined that she shall become the best dancer in Seville. Her father, like many Spaniards, holds more than one job. Though María's parents are poor, they manage to send her to Señor Realito's

Dancing Academy twice a week, to learn the twirls and heel stampings that make Spanish flamenco dancing so exciting.

Señor Carretero will tell you that Spain was once one of the world's great powers and, during her Golden Age, many Spanish writers and painters produced great works. The country has been the home of Celts, Phoenicians, Greeks, Carthaginians, Romans and other peoples who invaded Spain. In the fifth century, the Vithigoths invaded the land and ruled it for more than three centuries. The Moors swept into southern Spain from North Africa during the eighth century, and remained till they were driven out in 1492.

Today, the Alhambra, fortress of the sultans at Granada, the Mosque of Cordova, now a great cathedral, and the Alcázar in Seville with its lovely gardens are splendid and treasured reminders of the Moors. Some Spanish streets still have traces of the terrible Inquisition when Jews and Moslems were severely persecuted. Medieval synagogues were turned into churches when their Jewish worshipers were forced to flee the country. It is interesting that Hebrew symbols and letters can still be seen on them.

Many Spanish cities were made famous by their artists. The Greek painter, El Greco, so loved Toledo that he spent his entire life there. His great masterpieces and those of Velázquez, Murillo and Goya have helped to make the Prado in Madrid a leading art museum.

Still carrying the wounds of her civil war of 1936 and of the dictatorship that followed, Spain is trying hard to catch up with the progress and developments of the twentieth century. She puts on a bright face for visitors.

Dancing the Por Alegrías, a very popular Andalusian flamenco dance

Luxembourg

Imagine a country with 135 castles like those out of a storybook! One of the oldest and largest castles in Luxembourg is Vianden Castle. Its medieval massive bulk stands on a craggy hill overlooking the village of Vianden. Victor Hugo lived in this village during his exile from France and much of his time was spent exploring the ruins and ghostly turrets of the old castle. The Gothic doorway through which he wandered still stands and the great "salle de chevaliers," room of the knights, is just behind. Several hundred men could sit here comfortably.

Today it is not Victor Hugo, but eleven-year-old Jean Paul Folmer who wanders among the empty rooms and plays in the spellbinding halls. His father is the gatekeeper and the great castle has been Jean's home since he was born.

Vianden Castle, Jean Folmer's home

Jean loves to take visitors through the castle and show them the views of the valley and river below. The double defense walls, the dungeon, the echoing halls and the great cellar are exciting to see. While showing you about, Jean will tell you that the Grand Duchy of Luxembourg is smaller than the state of Rhode Island and is one of the tiniest countries in Europe. Letzeburgesch, which sounds like Flemish, is the widely-spoken language of the country, although French is the official tongue. Luxembourg gets its name from Lucilinburhuc, meaning "little town," and is a model democracy nestling on France's northern border between Belgium and Germany.

The people of Luxembourg love Americans who have twice helped to liberate their country from the Germans. Jean remembers the fine spring day when his uncle showed him through the rooms of the Alfa Hotel where some American generals lived for a time during World War II. Jean boasts proudly that he is probably the only boy in Luxembourg who bounced on the bed where Dwight D. Eisenhower once slept.

France

Some day you may take a trip to Europe and if you are like most tourists, you will hurry to Paris, the capital of France. There is so much to see there, but perhaps you will start by strolling down to the river Seine which winds through the heart of the city. There you will watch the fishermen and count the colorful barges as they make their slow journeys along the famous waterway. The benches along the walks at the water's edge are fine resting places and it won't be long before you are exercising your school French by asking the young son of a fisherman, "Quelle heure est-il?"

"It is almost twelve o'clock," Daniel Vidon will answer in proper English. After this exchange you will surely have made a friend. You will soon realize, too, that eight-year-old Daniel is just as eager to try his school English on you as you are to practice your school French on him. Daniel Vidon is wearing a smock and beret. He lives with his mother and father in a small apartment over one of the thousands of restaurants which make Paris a delightful place for lovers of good food. His father is owner and chef of the restaurant and his mother is the cashier.

Monsieur Vidon loves to fish in the Seine and, today, Daniel has come along to watch. His father caught a tiny sunfish, but promptly threw it back. Smiling, he will explain that fishermen in Paris really fish for sport, and not for the fish. Daniel has his hobby too. He likes to collect foreign stamps which he buys in the stamp market in the neighborhood of the Théâtre Marigny. The Vidons have invited you to lunch with them, but it is still early enough to show you some of the sights of Paris and to tell you something about France.

Not only has France been an important country in the formation of modern Europe, but it also played a significant part in the days when the United States was becoming an independent nation. During the American Revolution, France sent money, ships, troops and ammunition to the colonies. During the two World Wars, French and American forces fought side by side with other nations against oppression. The two countries have had close relations in literature, art and trade for years.

Soon you and Daniel and his father will pass the famous Garden of the Tuileries. Marie Antoinette and King Louis XVI were imprisoned, before their tragic deaths, in the palace which once stood on this site. Later, you will see the colorful flower markets of the Madeleine. From there, it is a short distance to the famous Opera House on the Avenue de l'Opéra. On this broad street, you will also see the Théâtre

Twig brooms clean streets in Paris

Français and the Palais Royal, its garden green with linden and elm trees. The Palais Royal was the center of fashionable society in the eighteenth century, and behind its closed doors were sown seeds of the French Revolution that changed the face of Europe.

Across the Rue de Rivoli, with its cool and shady arcades, is one of the most famous art museums in the world, the Louvre, once a palace. The treasures within its walls include such masterpieces as the portrait of the serene Mona Lisa, and the Greek statues of the Venus de Milo and the Winged Victory of Samothrace.

After a short walk along the right bank of the Seine you will soon come to an elaborate bridge called the Pont de Solferino and cross it to reach the left bank of Paris. You will be delighted by the bookstalls on the way to the section known as St. Germain des Prés. And soon, on the Rue Bonaparte, your curiosity will be aroused by some antique shops. Old-fashioned lampposts make you feel that you are living in the last century, when suddenly a burst of jazz from a trumpet in a cellar restaurant brings you back to the present. Daniel will tell you that many clubs and restaurants here feature American jazz music.

Dodging the hundreds of small French cars as they speed along the winding streets gives you a feeling of an industrialized and motorized France. But agriculture is the chief industry, not automobiles. France is one of the European leaders in the production of wheat. Barley, oats and rye are other important grains of the land. France's vineyards are plentiful and her wines are world-famous. Nearly 43 million people live in this country which is almost equal in territory to the states of Missouri, Iowa, Illinois and Indiana combined.

As you walk through ancient alleys, past modern shops, you will soon see the Cathedral of Notre Dame. It stands on an island in the middle of the Seine like some majestic ship of stone. It is here that great ceremonies celebrating victories and royal marriages took place. The coronation of Napoleon was held here too. In front of the cathedral stands the statue of Charlemagne, the great king of the Franks who admired learning and encouraged education.

Monsieur Vidon

Daniel will tell you about the Luxembourg Gardens with its Punch and Judy shows and rows of marble statues, and about the Métro, or subway, which millions of Parisians use daily. Daniel will surely point out the Eiffel Tower in the distance. It is one of the most famous structures in the world. Each year more than a million people come to see it and take the elevator up to the top to admire all of Paris around them. From the tower you can see many things, including the dome of the Hôtel des Invalides under which

Daniel has lunch in his father's restaurant

Napoleon is buried. The Hôtel also contains a military museum.

Daniel has also been to the provinces outside of Paris. He has seen the Roman remains in Provence, the Romanesque churches in Auvergne, the Gothic cathedrals of Ile de France and the romantic châteaux along the banks of the Loire. Daniel and his father have explored the palace of Versailles, near Paris. It was built for Louis XIV and has since served as a place for many world conferences. Daniel also visited the Palace of Fontainebleau, well known for its rooms decorated with frescoes and plaster carvings. Napoleon signed his abdication here before going into exile. Daniel has been to Château-Thierry where American soldiers fought in World War I.

One special event that Daniel remembers is the visit he and his father made to the Forest of Paimpont. This is the same forest where, so the legend goes, the magician Merlin and the enchantress Vivian lived during the time of King Arthur and his Knights of the Round Table. Some people in the countryside still believe that the forest is haunted.

Next summer Daniel has been promised a trip to colorful Marseilles, France's chief port on the Mediterranean. From there it is not far to the French Riviera which stretches from Toulon to the Italian border. This is the famous Côte d'Azur, a beach and country area which attracts thousands of people who come to swim in the blue sea, and enjoy the sun and sea breezes.

The famous Mardi Gras carnival in Nice begins two weeks before Lent, and the French Côte d'Azur is decked with flowers, confetti and streamers. Daniel, however, is more interested in skindiving. The water here resembles the ocean around southern Florida, and has an abundance of exotic fish and other sea curiosities.

It is lunchtime and in a little while, you will arrive at the restaurant of Daniel's father. Monsieur

Vidon, wearing his big white chef's hat, will prepare Steak à l'Améri-caine in your honor. It is none other than a hamburger, but as a French touch, Monsieur Vidon will add a fried egg on top. Daniel agrees, with his mouth full, that this is his idea of a very successful hamburger, and you will, too.

"Paris is a world unto itself," said Charles V in the sixteenth century. As you walk on worn stones that once held processions of kings, queens, artists and scholars, and watch the sun light up palaces and parks, you may agree with Daniel and King Charles that Paris is the most exciting and most beautiful city in Europe.

Bookstalls line the quays along the Seine. In the background looms the majestic Louvre